Cake

[keyk] *(pl -s), noun:*

100 essential recipes

Cake

[keyk] *(pl -s), noun:*

....

100 essential recipes

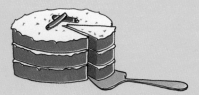

spruce

An Hachette UK Company
www.hachette.co.uk

First published in Great Britain in 2013 by Spruce
A division of Octopus Publishing Group Ltd
Endeavour House, 189 Shaftesbury Avenue, London, WC2H 8JY
www.octopusbooks.co.uk
www.octopusbooksusa.com

Distributed in the US by Hachette Book Group USA
237 Park Avenue, New York NY 10017 USA

Distributed in Canada by Canadian Manda Group
165 Dufferin Street, Toronto, Ontario, Canada M6K 3H6

ISBN 978 1 84601 420 8

Printed and bound in china

10 9 8 7 6 5 4 3 2 1

CONSULTANT PUBLISHER Sarah Ford
COPY EDITOR Jo Richardson
DESIGN Eoghan O'Brien & Clare Barber
ILLUSTRATOR Abigail Read
PRODUCTION Caroline Alberti

CONTENTS

INTRODUCTION

A piece of cake is one of our most treasured comfort foods. Sweet and indulgent, it fills the gap between meals perfectly, and it's a treat elevated to new heights when the cake is homemade. This book aims to encourage all cooks to get baking—the recipes are all easy to make and range from firm favorites to slightly quirkier creations for confirmed "cake-aholics." Some are best served absolutely fresh, preferably still slightly warm, while others are good keepers, ideal for feeding a crowd.

ESSENTIAL INGREDIENTS

To ensure a good result, choose only premium ingredients for your cakes.

FATS

It's always best to use unsalted butter because it imparts a good flavor and is free from the additives that many spreads and margarines contain, even if the package specifies that they can be used for baking. If you run out of unsalted butter, the quantity can be topped up or substituted with lightly salted butter, but avoid using regular salted butter because the salty flavor will affect the taste of the cake. Margarines and nondairy spreads can be used if necessary, but check they are suitable for baking before you buy. A few of the recipes use olive oil as an alternative to butter. Choose one with a mild or medium flavor so that it doesn't dominate the other ingredients.

SUGAR

Superfine sugar is the first choice for sponge and lighter cakes, but if you can't find it, grind regular granulated sugar in a food processor for a few seconds until it is finer in texture—let the dust settle before opening the processor. Dark and light brown sugar and raw brown sugar give an extra boost to robust-flavored cakes, and combine well with chocolate, spices, and molasses. Some brown sugars may harden during storage, so to make them possible to bake with, put the package in the microwave and give it short bursts on medium power until the sugar has softened.

EGGS

For the best color and taste use good-quality, well-flavored eggs, preferably free-range. If you store eggs in the refrigerator, try to remember to remove them well before baking, as they will give more volume and are less likely to curdle in creamed mixtures when they are at room temperature.

FLOUR

Self-rising flour is the type of flour most widely used in cake making because it already includes a leavening agent. Some self-rising flours are sold specially for cake baking—they are sifted more finely and are designed to give a lighter sponge. A few recipes in this book substitute whole wheat flour for some of the quantity of white flour, in order to give a more textured, wholesome flavor. If you prefer to bake with whole wheat flour, you can use it in any recipe in place of some of the white flour.

SPECIAL EQUIPMENT

You will probably already have much of the equipment you need to make most basic cakes, but the following items are essential.

MIXERS

An electric mixer takes all the effort out of cake making. A stand mixer with wire whip and flat beater attachments is very handy if you make a lot of cakes, particularly if you are working with larger quantities of ingredients. Use the flat beater for creamed mixtures and the whip for fatless sponges and Genoese cakes. A large-capacity food processor is good for creamed mixtures, and a small, electric hand mixer is a useful and affordable all-round kitchen tool. Wire whisks and rotary whisks can be used for any cakes, but the job will take a bit longer and be much harder work!

CAKE PANS

Strong, sturdy, deep cake pans will last for years, so it's worth investing in a few sizes if you intend to bake regularly. The most frequently used pans in this book are 7-inch and 8-inch round cake pans. Square pans can easily be substituted, but always use a slightly smaller size—for example, use a 6-inch square in place of a 7-inch round, or a 7-inch square instead of an 8-inch round. A slightly larger pan can be used if you don't have the right size (the cake will be slightly shallower and the cooking time may be slightly less), but avoid using a smaller pan because the batter may spill over during baking or sink in the center.

Most cake pans are available with a loose bottom, which makes it easier to remove the cake from the pan. A pan with a loose bottom is best for recipes that have a soft fruity or crumbly topping that may get damaged if the cake were inverted. Muffin pans, round and rectangular shallow pans, and loaf pans are also useful for baking. Nonstick versions are widely available and tend to be harder wearing, as they are not prone to rust. Silicone rubber flexible molds are now available for small cakes, but they come in a more limited range of sizes. There is no need to grease the molds, and the baked cakes can be easily popped out of them.

Before baking, line pans with parchment paper if the recipe requires it (see below). Lining nonstick pans is not essential but does make the cakes easier to unmold.

LINING CAKE PANS

To line cake pans, use parchment paper and brush the bottom and sides of the pan with melted butter before you start lining. Most cakes need a completely lined pan, both bottom and sides, but some need only the bottom lined with a circle of paper. See the individual recipes for directions on how to line the pans.

ROUND PANS

Using the pan as a guide, draw a circle on the parchment paper and cut it out. Cut strips of paper a little wider than the height of the pan, fold over a lip approximately ½-inch wide, and snip it at intervals. Brush the side and bottom of the pan with melted butter.

Fit the paper around the side of the pan so that the lip sits flat on the bottom. Press the circle of paper into the pan bottom and brush all of the parchment paper with more melted butter.

SQUARE PANS

Use the same technique as for round pans, but once you have cut the square bottom and strips, you need to make snips only where the paper fits into the corners of the pan.

LOAF PANS

A long strip of parchment paper that covers the bottom and long sides is usually sufficient for lining a loaf pan and makes lifting the cake out very easy. If the pan needs lining fully, add another two strips of paper at the short ends.

RECTANGULAR SHALLOW AND JELLY ROLL PANS

Cut a rectangle of parchment paper that is 3 inches longer and wider than the cake pan.

Press the paper into the greased pan, snipping it at the corners to make sure that it fits neatly.

ROUND SHALLOW PANS

Draw and cut out circles of parchment paper, using the pans as a guide. Grease the pans and line their bottoms with the paper circles. Alternatively, grease the pans, tip in a little flour, and tilt each pan so that the flour coats the bottom and side. Tap out the excess flour.

RING AND BUNDT PANS

Brush the pan thoroughly with melted butter. Tip a little flour into the bottom of the pan and tilt it until the bottom and sides are evenly coated with flour. Then tap out the excess flour.

CAKE-MAKING METHODS

There are several basic techniques used in cake making. Being aware of the different processes involved will ensure consistently good results.

CREAMED CAKES

Creaming is the traditional method of making sandwich cakes and buttery sponges. The butter must be very soft (soften it in a microwave if you forget to leave it out of the refrigerator) so that it has a smooth, creamy consistency when it is beaten with the sugar. When it's thoroughly creamed, the butter and sugar mixture should be much paler in color than the butter alone was, and it should also be very soft. This stage of the process is often described as "light and fluffy." The beaten eggs are added a little at a

time. If the eggs are added too quickly, the batter will curdle, which may affect the texture of the cake. If this happens, add a little of the flour before finally folding in the remaining flour with a large metal spoon.

WHIPPED CAKES

The whipping method is used to make an aerated, fatless sponge. It's the air trapped in the batter when the eggs and sugar are beaten together that gives a whipped cake its volume. A whipped mixture is more delicate than a creamed mixture, so take care throughout the mixing process to keep it aerated and light. Placing the bowl over a saucepan of simmering water will help to speed up whipping. Flour is folded in to stabilize the mixture, and it's important to do this as gently as possible so that the foamy consistency is not lost. All-purpose flour is used in whipped cakes because there is no need for additional leavening agents.

MELTED CAKES

This quick and easy method is used for cakes like gingerbread where the butter and sugars are melted together in a saucepan before being combined with the dry ingredients. These cakes have a dense but moist texture and rely on baking powder and baking soda to make them rise. It's important to bake the cake as soon as the ingredients are mixed together because the leavening agents are activated when the wet and dry ingredients are combined. Melted cakes keep well and often improve in flavor and texture if they are wrapped and stored for a couple of days before being eaten.

RUBBED-IN CAKES

Used for muffins, crumble cakes, and rock buns, this method resembles the one used for homemade pie dough. The butter is rubbed into the flour (sometimes with other dry ingredients like oats) with the fingertips or, more conveniently, in a food processor, before the remaining ingredients are added. With the exception of crumble cakes, rubbed-in cakes contain a small proportion of butter and usually go stale quickly. They are generally best eaten on the day they are made or, if kept for longer, reheated before serving.

SOME BASIC TECHNIQUES

Here are some of the standard techniques that crop up repeatedly in the recipes.

SOFTENING BUTTER

All cakes made using the creamed method require softened butter. This is most easily done in the microwave, because few of us will remember to remove the butter from the refrigerator well in advance of a baking session. Soften it in a few short bursts, checking each time. The butter should be soft enough to push into it with your finger.

MELTING CHOCOLATE

Break the chocolate into pieces and place in a heatproof bowl. Rest the bowl over a saucepan of gently simmering water, making sure the bottom of the bowl doesn't come into contact with the water. Once the chocolate starts to melt, turn off the heat and let stand until it has completely melted, stirring once or twice until no lumps remain. To melt chocolate in the microwave, use a microwave-safe bowl and melt the chocolate on medium power in 1- to 2-minute spurts, checking frequently. If you are melting chocolate with other ingredients—butter, milk, or cream, for example—keep a close eye on the mixture because the high fat content will speed up the melting.

FOLDING IN

Flours, flavorings, melted butter, or whipped egg whites are usually "folded" gently into creamed cake and sponge mixes rather than being beaten in. This is because the aim is to keep the mixture

light and aerated. Push a large metal spoon down into the mixture and lift it up and over the ingredients you have added so that you start folding them together. Continue mixing the ingredients together in this way, using a very gentle action and turning the bowl slowly with your other hand until the ingredients are just blended. When you are adding whipped egg whites to a mixture, fold in about a quarter of the quantity before adding the remainder. The first batch will be useful in lightening the mixture, particularly if it's very firm, which will make it easier for you to fold in the rest of the eggs.

CHECKING THAT A CAKE IS COOKED

Try not to be impatient when you are waiting for a cake to bake—no matter how strong the desire to eat it might be! Repeatedly opening the oven door, allowing a rush of cold air into the oven, may cause the cake to sink in the center. You should check that a cake is cooked shortly before it's due to come out of the oven. If it's slightly domed in the center, has a baked color, and doesn't "give" in the center when lightly touched with a flattened hand, it's ready. Fruit cakes and other deep cakes can be tested by pushing a fine skewer into the center—it should come out just clean. If there is still raw mixture clinging to the skewer, return to the oven for a little longer. Exceptions to this rule are really moist chocolate cakes and brownies. Brownies in particular should feel very loose under the crust because of the high sugar content, but they will become firmer as they cool.

COOLING CAKES ON A WIRE RACK

Most sponge cakes should be removed from the pan as soon as you have taken them out of the oven. Loosen the cake sides with a knife to help release it if you haven't lined the sides of the pan, and be careful because the hot sponge will fall apart easily. Remove rich fruit cakes from the pan only when completely cool.

JAMMY ALMOND SPONGE CAKE P31

CLASSIC & EVERYDAY CAKES

VICTORIA SANDWICH

A true British classic, this buttery sponge cake can be served sandwiched with a little jam or, for a more elaborate occasion, with some whipped cream and fresh raspberries.

SERVES 8

- Vegetable oil, for oiling
- 1 cup plus 2 tablespoons (2¼ sticks) unsalted butter, softened
- 1¼ cups superfine sugar, plus extra for serving
- 4 eggs, lightly beaten
- 2 cups self-rising flour
- Pinch of salt
- 1 tablespoon milk
- 1 teaspoon vanilla extract
- Raspberry or strawberry jam, for filling

1. Preheat the oven to 350°F. Oil and line the bottom of two 8-inch round shallow cake pans.

2. In a stand mixer, beat all the cake ingredients together on medium speed for 1 minute, or until evenly mixed.

3. Divide the batter equally among the prepared pans and bake in the oven for 25–30 minutes, or until risen and firm to the touch. Let cool in the pans for 5 minutes, then transfer to a wire rack to cool completely.

4. Sandwich the sponges together with jam, dust the top with superfine sugar, and serve.

TIP

- For chocolate sponge cake, follow the method above but replace a ⅓ cup plus 1 tablespoon of the flour with unsweetened cocoa. Bake as normal. Fill the cake with a simple chocolate frosting and dust with superfine sugar.

BUTTERY BRETON CAKE

MAKES 25 SQUARES

- 1¾ cups self-rising flour, plus extra for dusting
- 1½ cups confectioners' sugar
- 2 tablespoons vanilla sugar, plus extra for dusting
- ¾ cup plus 2 tablespoons (1¾ sticks) lightly salted butter, chilled and diced, plus extra for greasing
- 5 egg yolks, plus 1 beaten egg, to glaze
- ½ cup strawberry jam

1. Preheat the oven to 375°F. Grease and line a 7–7½-inch square shallow baking pan.

2. Sift the flour and confectioners' sugar into a food processor, add the vanilla sugar and butter, and process until the mixture resembles coarse bread crumbs. Add the egg yolks and process again to make a thick paste. Wrap in plastic wrap and chill for at least 3 hours or overnight.

3. Press half of the dough into the prepared pan, spreading it into the corners with your fingers so that it forms an even layer. Spread the jam over the dough, leaving ½ inch clear around the edges.

4. Roll out the remaining dough on a floured work surface to the same dimensions as the pan and lift into place. Press down gently and brush with beaten egg.

5. Bake in the oven for 40–45 minutes, until risen and deep golden. Let cool in the pan, then transfer to a flat plate or board. Dust lightly with vanilla sugar and cut into squares.

POUND CAKE WITH BUTTER SYRUP

Pound cake is a very old recipe; it originally used a pound of each ingredient—butter, sugar, eggs, and flour. This scaled-down version has a wonderful butter glaze.

SERVES 10

- 1½ cups (3 sticks) unsalted butter, softened, plus extra, melted, for greasing
- 1½ cups superfine sugar
- 2 teaspoons finely grated lemon zest
- 1½ cups all-purpose flour, plus extra for dusting
- 1 cup potato flour
- 1½ teaspoons baking powder
- 6 eggs, beaten
- 2 tablespoons milk

Glaze
- ½ cup superfine sugar
- 4 tablespoons (½ stick) unsalted butter
- 4 tablespoons water
- 1 teaspoon vanilla extract

1. Preheat the oven to 350°F. Brush a 10-inch bundt pan twice with melted butter and lightly dust with flour, tapping out the excess.

2. In a bowl, beat the butter and sugar together until pale and fluffy. Stir in the lemon zest. Sift the all-purpose flour, potato flour, and baking powder into a separate bowl.

3. Gradually beat the eggs into the creamed mixture, a little at a time, beating well after each addition and adding a little of the flour if the batter begins to curdle. Fold in the remaining flour mixture with a large metal spoon, then stir in the milk until well mixed.

4. Spoon the batter into the prepared pan and level the surface. Bake in the oven for 45–55 minutes, or until a toothpick inserted into the center comes out clean. Ease the cake away from the side of the pan, then let cool in the pan for 10 minutes before turning out onto a wire rack.

5. Make the glaze. In a saucepan, gently heat the sugar, butter, and water, stirring, until the butter melts. Simmer gently for 3 minutes, then remove from the heat and stir in the vanilla extract. Pour the butter glaze evenly over the warm cake and let cool completely. Serve in slices.

STICKY TOFFEE CAKE

Not many cake lovers will resist the temptation to come back for more of this gorgeous treat. Like the pudding that it imitates, it's wickedly good when served with cream!

SERVES 10

- ¾ cup pitted dried dates, chopped
- ⅔ cup water
- ½ cup plus 1 tablespoon (1 stick plus 1 tablespoon) unsalted butter, softened, plus extra for greasing
- ½ cup superfine sugar
- 2 teaspoons vanilla extract
- 3 eggs

- 1⅓ cups plus 1 tablespoon self-rising flour
- 1 teaspoon baking powder

Topping
- ⅔ cup heavy cream
- ¾ cup plus 2 tablespoons light brown sugar
- 5 tablespoons (½ stick plus 1 tablespoon) unsalted butter

1. In a small saucepan, bring the dates and water to a boil. Reduce the heat and gently cook for 5 minutes, or until the dates are soft and pulpy. Turn into a bowl to cool.

2. Make the topping. In the cleaned-out pan, gently heat all the topping ingredients until the sugar dissolves. Bring to a boil and let bubble for 6–8 minutes, or until thickened. Let cool.

3. Meanwhile, preheat the oven to 350°F. Grease and line a 7-inch round springform or loose-bottom cake pan. Grease the paper.

4. In a bowl, beat the butter, sugar, vanilla extract, eggs, flour, and baking powder together until smooth and creamy. Stir in the date purée and a heaping ⅓ cup of the topping.

5. Turn the batter into the prepared pan and level the surface. Bake in the oven for about 40 minutes, or until just firm.

6. Remove from the oven and tip the remaining topping over the cake. Bake for an additional 20 minutes. Transfer to a wire rack, leaving the lining paper attached until the cake has cooled.

GINGERBREAD

Rich, moist gingerbread keeps well and should be stored for several days before eating, as the flavor develops with time.

SERVES 24
- Vegetable oil, for oiling
- 4 cups self-rising flour
- 1 tablespoon ground ginger
- ½ teaspoon baking soda
- ½ teaspoon salt
- ¾ cup plus 2 tablespoons light brown sugar
- ¾ cup (1½ sticks) unsalted butter
- ½ cup blackstrap molasses
- ½ cup dark corn syrup
- 1¼ cups milk
- 1 egg, lightly beaten

1. Preheat the oven to 325°F. Oil and line the bottom of an 12- x 8-inch baking pan.

2. Sift the flour, ginger, baking soda, and salt into a bowl.

3. In a saucepan, gently heat the sugar, butter, molasses, and corn syrup until the butter melts and the sugar dissolves.

4. Pour the liquid into the dry ingredients with the milk and egg and beat with a wooden spoon until smooth.

5. Pour the batter into the prepared pan and bake in the oven for 1¼ hours, or until a toothpick inserted into the center comes out clean. Let cool in the pan for 10 minutes, then turn out onto a wire rack to cool completely.

TIP

- To store, wrap the cooled cake in aluminum foil and place in an airtight container.

LEMON DRIZZLE CAKE

Ask anyone to list their favorite cakes and this will almost certainly be one of them. Intensely lemony and with an irresistibly sugary crust, this version is one of the best.

SERVES 8-10

- 1 cup (2 sticks) unsalted butter, softened, plus extra for greasing
- 1 cup plus 2 tablespoons superfine sugar
- Finely grated zest of 3 lemons and ⅓ cup plus 1 tablespoon juice
- 4 eggs, beaten
- 2 cups self-rising flour
- 1 teaspoon baking powder
- ¾ cup ground almonds
- ½ cup granulated sugar

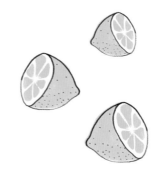

1. Preheat the oven to 350°F. Grease and line the bottom of an 8-inch round or 7-inch square cake pan. Grease the paper.

2. In a large bowl, beat the butter, superfine sugar, and lemon zest together until light and fluffy. Gradually beat in the eggs, a little at a time, beating well after each addition and adding a little of the flour if the batter starts to curdle. Sift in the flour and baking powder, then add the ground almonds and 2 tablespoons of the lemon juice, and gently fold them in with a large metal spoon.

3. Turn the batter into the prepared pan and level the surface. Bake in the oven for about 45 minutes, or until just firm and a toothpick inserted into the center comes out clean.

4. Meanwhile, mix the remaining lemon juice with the granulated sugar.

5. Transfer the cooked cake to a wire rack. While still hot, stir the lemon mixture well and spoon over the cake. As the cake cools, the syrup will sink into the cake, leaving a sugary crust.

POPPY SEED & ORANGE BUNDT CAKE

If you don't have a traditional bundt pan, use a plain or fluted ring pan for this light and airy cake.

SERVES 10
- ⅔ cup (1 stick plus 2½ tablespoons) unsalted butter, softened, plus extra for greasing
- 1¼ cups superfine sugar
- 3 eggs, beaten
- 3 tablespoons poppy seeds
- Finely grated zest and juice of 1 orange
- 2⅓ cups self-rising flour, plus extra for dusting
- 1 teaspoon baking powder
- 1 cup buttermilk
- Scant ⅓ cup whiskey-flavored orange marmalade
- Glacé Icing (see page 150)

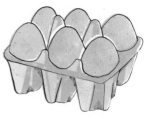

1. Preheat the oven to 325°F. Grease a 6 ¼-cup bundt or ring pan and lightly dust with flour, tapping out the excess.

2. In a large bowl, beat the butter and sugar together until light and fluffy. Gradually beat in the eggs, a little at a time, beating well after each addition. Stir in the poppy seeds, orange zest, and half of the orange juice. Sift in the flour and baking powder, add the buttermilk, and fold in with a large metal spoon until just combined.

3. Turn the batter into the prepared pan and level the surface. Bake in the oven for 45 minutes, or until risen and just firm and a toothpick inserted into the center comes out clean. Let cool in the pan.

4. Turn the cooled cake out onto a plate. In a small saucepan, gently heat the marmalade with the remaining orange juice until it melts, then brush over the surface of the cake. Spoon the glacé icing over the top so that it trickles down the sides.

CARROT CAKE

This is a light, spongy carrot cake with the subtle addition of ginger and orange. Even when smothered with the tangy cream cheese frosting, it remains fresh and clean tasting.

SERVES 10-12

- I cup (2 sticks) unsalted butter, softened, plus extra for greasing
- I cup plus 2 tablespoons light brown sugar
- 4 eggs
- Finely grated zest of I orange
- I⅓ cups plus I tablespoon self-rising flour
- I teaspoon baking powder
- I cup ground hazelnuts
- 4 drained pieces stem ginger in syrup (about 2½ oz), chopped
- 2¾ cups finely grated carrots
- ½ cup raisins
- Cream Cheese Frosting (see page 151)
- Toasted hazelnuts, roughly chopped, to decorate

1. Preheat the oven to 350°F. Grease and line an 8-inch round cake pan.

2. In a large bowl, beat the butter, sugar, eggs, orange zest, flour, baking powder, ground hazelnuts, and ginger together until smooth and creamy. Stir in the carrots and raisins until evenly combined.

TIP

- If you can't find ground hazelnuts, grind whole blanched ones in a food processor, or you can use ground almonds.

3. Turn the batter into the prepared pan and level the surface. Bake in the oven for about 1 hour, or until just firm and a toothpick inserted into the center comes out clean. Transfer to a wire rack to cool.

4. Spread the frosting over the top and side of the cake with a palette knife, then decorate with chopped toasted hazelnuts.

PLUM POLENTA CAKE

Instant polenta (cornmeal) and ground almonds are used instead of flour in this incredibly moist cake. Apricots make a good alternative to plums.

SERVES 10

- 1¾ cups instant polenta (cornmeal)
- 2 teaspoons baking powder
- 1 cup ground almonds
- 1 cup plus 2 tablespoons unrefined superfine sugar, plus an extra 2 tablespoons
- ⅔ cup sour cream
- ⅓ cup plus 1 tablespoon mild olive oil, plus extra for oiling
- Finely grated zest of 2 lemons and 4 tablespoons juice
- 3 eggs
- ¾ pound red plums
- 6 tablespoons clear honey

1. Preheat the oven to 350°F. Oil a 9-inch round springform or loose-bottom cake pan.

2. In a bowl, combine the polenta, baking powder, ground almonds, and the 1 cup plus 2 tablespoons sugar.

3. In a separate bowl, beat the sour cream, oil, lemon zest and 1 tablespoon of the juice, and the eggs together. Add to the dry ingredients and stir well until evenly combined.

4. Turn the batter into the prepared pan. Remove the pits from the plums, then cut the plums into quarters. Scatter over the surface of the cake in an even layer and sprinkle with the remaining 2 tablespoons sugar.

5. Bake in the oven for about 1 hour, or until risen and just firm and a toothpick inserted into the cake between the plums comes out clean.

6. Mix the honey with the remaining lemon juice and drizzle over the warm cake. Let cool in the pan.

MOIST RICOTTA CAKE

This cake is delicious served with coffee after a light meal. If you think of it in time, soak the raisins overnight so they've plenty of time to plump.

SERVES 9-10

- ⅔ cup raisins
- 3 tablespoons Marsala
- ¾ cup (1½ sticks) unsalted butter, softened, plus extra for greasing
- ¾ cup plus 2 tablespoons superfine sugar
- 1 cup ricotta cheese
- 1 teaspoon vanilla extract
- 3 eggs, separated
- 1¼ cups self-rising flour
- 1 teaspoon baking powder
- Confectioners' sugar, for dusting

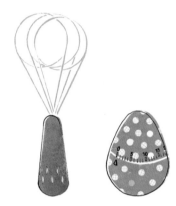

1. Preheat the oven to 350°F. Grease and line the bottom of a 7-inch square or 8-inch round cake pan.

2. In a small bowl, combine the raisins and Marsala, cover, and let soak for 30 minutes.

3. In a large bowl, beat the butter and superfine sugar together until light and fluffy, then beat in the ricotta, vanilla extract, and egg yolks. Stir in the soaked raisins and any unabsorbed Marsala.

4. In a separate, thoroughly clean bowl, whip the egg whites with an electric hand mixer until peaking.

5. Fold a quarter of the whipped egg whites into the cake batter with a large metal spoon to lighten it, then fold in the remainder. Sift the flour and baking powder into the bowl and fold in until combined.

6. Turn the batter into the prepared pan and level the surface. Bake in the oven for 40 minutes, or until just firm to the touch. Transfer to a wire rack to cool. Serve dusted with plenty of confectioners' sugar.

CHERRY JELLY ROLL

A light-as-air sponge is rolled up around a fruity filling, in this case cherry sauce. If you're short of time, a thick layer of good raspberry or strawberry jam makes an easy alternative.

SERVES 8

- Butter, for greasing
- ⅔ cup superfine sugar, plus extra for dusting
- 3 large eggs
- 1 cup all-purpose flour
- 1 tablespoon water

Filling
- 15-ounce can pitted dark sweet cherries
- 1½ teaspoons cornstarch
- 2 tablespoons superfine sugar

1. Preheat the oven to 400°F. Grease and line a 13- x 9-inch jelly roll pan.

2. Make the filling. Drain the cherries, reserving the juice. In a small saucepan, blend ⅓ cup plus 1 tablespoon of the juice with the cornstarch and the 2 tablespoons sugar. Roughly chop the cherries, add to the pan, and cook gently for 3–4 minutes until thickened. Let cool.

3. In a large heatproof bowl set over a saucepan of gently simmering water, whip the sugar and eggs together with an electric hand mixer until pale, creamy, and thick enough for the beaters to leave a trail when lifted from the bowl. Remove from the heat and beat for an additional 2 minutes.

4. Sift in half of the flour and gently fold in with a large metal spoon. Sift in the remaining flour and fold in. Sprinkle over the water and fold in.

5. Turn the batter into the prepared pan and gently spread into the corners. Bake in the oven for 10–12 minutes, or until just firm.

6. Meanwhile, sprinkle a sheet of parchment paper with a little sugar.

7. Quickly turn the cooked sponge out onto the sugared paper. Carefully peel off the lining paper. Spread with the filling and roll up, starting from a short side and using the paper to help you. Let cool, seam-side down, on a wire rack.

BLACKBERRY MUFFIN SLICE

Light in texture and not too sweet, this is a good breakfast or mid-morning cake, served sliced and buttered. It's best eaten freshly made, preferably slightly warm.

SERVES 6-8

- 7 tablespoons (½ stick plus 3 tablespoons) unsalted butter, melted, plus extra for greasing
- ¾ cup milk
- 1 egg
- 2 cups all-purpose flour
- 2 teaspoons baking powder
- ¾ cup superfine sugar, plus extra for dusting
- ⅓ cup rolled oats
- ⅔ cup fresh blackberries

1. Preheat the oven to 350°F. Grease and line a 1-pound loaf pan so that the paper comes about ½ inch above the rim. Grease the paper.

2. In a bowl, beat the butter, milk, and egg together. In another bowl, sift in the flour and baking powder, then stir in the sugar, oats, and half of the blackberries. Stir in the milk mixture until it is only just combined.

3. Turn the batter into the prepared pan and scatter with the remaining blackberries. Bake in the oven for 50–60 minutes, or until well risen, golden, and firm to the touch.

4. Let cool in the pan for 5 minutes, then transfer to a wire rack and sprinkle with a little extra sugar. Serve warm or cold.

JAMMY ALMOND
SPONGE CAKE

Use your favorite jam in this almond pastry sheet cake. This would be perfect for cutting into squares and selling at your next cake sale.

SERVES 20

- 8-ounce package prepared pie dough
- ½ cup jam, such as raspberry
- 1 cup (2 sticks) butter, softened, plus extra for greasing
- 1 cup superfine sugar
- 4 eggs
- 1½ cups ground almonds
- Scant ½ cup all-purpose flour, plus extra for dusting
- 1 cup slivered almonds, lightly toasted

1. Preheat the oven to 350°F. Lightly grease a 13- x 9-inch baking pan.

2. Roll out the pie dough on a lightly floured work surface and lift into the prepared pan so that it covers the bottom and comes up the sides, overhanging slightly. Cover the bottom with an even layer of jam.

3. In a large bowl, beat the butter and sugar together until pale and creamy. Add the eggs, one at a time, beating well and adding a spoonful of the ground almonds after each addition. Fold in the remaining ground almonds and flour with a large metal spoon.

4. Place spoonfuls of the batter over the jam layer, spreading evenly with the back of the spoon. Sprinkle over the slivered almonds. Bake in the oven for about 35 minutes, or until firm and golden. Trim the pastry.

5. Let cool slightly in the pan, then cut into squares and lift with a metal spatula onto a wire rack to cool completely.

BANANA TOFFEE SHEET CAKE

- -

This sheet cake has a moist, banana sponge base, topped with layers of toffee sauce, fresh bananas, and softly whipped cream—and what better way to finish it all off than with a dusting of grated chocolate.

SERVES 12-16

- ¾ cup (1½ sticks) butter, softened, plus extra for greasing
- ¾ cup light brown sugar
- 3 eggs, beaten
- 1½ cups self-rising flour
- ¼ teaspoon ground cinnamon
- 1 teaspoon baking powder
- 5 bananas, 2 ripe and mashed and 3 sliced
- 1–2 tablespoons milk
- 1 cup heavy cream
- ⅓ cup coarsely grated milk chocolate (optional)

Toffee sauce
- 1⅓ cups sweetened condensed milk
- 5 tablespoons (½ stick plus 1 tablespoon) butter
- ⅓ cup superfine sugar

1. Preheat the oven to 350°F. Grease and line the bottom of a deep 13- x 9-inch baking pan.

2. In a large bowl, beat the butter and sugar together until light and fluffy. Add the eggs, flour, ground cinnamon, and baking powder and beat until well combined. Fold in the mashed bananas and milk.

3. Turn the batter into the prepared pan and level the surface. Bake in the oven for about 30 minutes, or until risen and springy to the touch. Let cool in the pan for 5–10 minutes, then turn onto a wire rack. Peel off the lining paper and let cool completely.

4. Make the toffee sauce. In a saucepan, gently heat the condensed milk, butter, and sugar, stirring frequently, until the sugar dissolves. Simmer gently until thick and golden. Set aside to cool a little—it needs to be warm enough to spread, but not too hot.

5. Spread the sauce over the sponge, let cool, then top with the bananas.

6. Whip the cream until it forms soft peaks and cover the banana-toffee layer. Sprinkle with the grated chocolate, if using, and serve in thick slabs.

COCONUT & PINEAPPLE SHEET CAKE

Bring a taste of the Tropics to your kitchen with this coconut and pineapple cake. The deliciously moist sponge cake contrasts perfectly with the crisp crumble topping.

SERVES 12-16

- ½ cup plus 1 tablespoon (1 stick plus 1 tablespoon) butter, plus extra for greasing
- 1 cup superfine sugar
- 3 eggs
- 1⅔ cups all-purpose flour
- 2 teaspoons baking powder
- ¼ teaspoon salt
- ⅔ cup crème fraîche or equal quantities sour cream and whipping cream
- ⅓ cup shredded dried coconut
- 1 cup fresh or canned pineapple chunks

Crumble
- ¼ cup all-purpose flour
- ½ cup dark brown sugar
- 2 tablespoons shredded dried coconut
- 3½ tablespoons (¼ stick plus 1½ tablespoons) butter, softened

1. Preheat the oven to 350°F. Grease and line a deep 9-inch square cake pan.

2. Make the crumble topping. In a bowl, combine the flour, sugar, and coconut, then rub in the butter with the fingertips until the mixture is lumpy. Set aside.

3. In a large bowl, beat the butter and sugar together until pale and creamy. Add the eggs, one at a time, beating well after each addition. Fold in the flour, baking powder, and salt and then the crème fraîche or sour cream and cream mixture and coconut with a large metal spoon.

4. Turn the batter into the prepared pan and scatter over the pineapple chunks and crumble topping. Bake in the oven for 1 hour 20 minutes, or until firm and golden and a toothpick inserted into the center comes out clean.

5. Let cool in the pan, then carefully lift out using the lining paper. Peel off the lining paper and cut the cake into squares. Serve slightly warm or cool.

FRUIT & NUT CUPCAKES P49

FRUITY & NUTTY

PEAR, CARDAMOM & RAISIN CAKE

SERVES 10

- ½ cup (1 stick) unsalted butter, softened, plus extra for greasing
- ½ cup light brown sugar
- 2 eggs, lightly beaten
- 2 cups self-rising flour
- 1 teaspoon ground cardamom
- 4 tablespoons milk
- 1 pound pears, peeled, cored, and thinly sliced
- ¾ cup golden raisins
- 1 tablespoon clear honey

1. Preheat the oven to 325°F. Grease and line a 2-pound loaf pan.

2. In a bowl, beat the butter and sugar together until pale and creamy. Gradually beat in the eggs, a little at a time, beating well after each addition. Sift the flour and cardamom together, then fold into the creamed mixture with the milk using a large metal spoon.

3. Reserve about one-third of the pear slices and coarsely chop the rest. Fold the chopped pears into the creamed mixture with the golden raisins.

4. Spoon the batter into the prepared pan and level the surface. Arrange the reserved pear slices along the center of the cake, pressing them in gently.

5. Bake in the oven for 1¼–1½ hours, or until a toothpick inserted into the center comes out clean.

6. Let cool in the pan for 10 minutes, then lift out using the lining paper. Transfer to a wire rack, peel off the lining paper, and let cool completely. Transfer to a serving plate and drizzle with the honey.

BANANA & WALNUT SPICE CAKE

This cake is made in a bundt pan, an ornate ring pan that has become very popular in many baking circles, but you can easily use a plain ring pan if you prefer.

SERVES 8-10

- Vegetable oil, for oiling
- 1 cup plus 2 tablespoons (2¼ sticks) unsalted butter, softened
- 1¼ cups light brown sugar
- 4 eggs, beaten
- 2 cups self-rising flour
- 1½ teaspoons baking powder
- 1 teaspoon apple pie spice
- Pinch of salt
- 3 bananas, mashed
- ⅔ cup walnuts, toasted and finely chopped
- Confectioners' sugar, for dusting

1. Preheat the oven to 325°F. Oil a 10-inch bundt pan.

2. Place the butter, brown sugar, and eggs in a stand mixer. Sift in the flour, baking powder, spice, and salt and beat on medium speed for 1 minute until smooth. Stir in the bananas and walnuts.

TIP

- To make by hand, in a bowl, beat the butter and sugar together until light and fluffy, then gradually beat in the eggs, a little at a time, beating well after each addition. Fold in the remaining ingredients with a large metal spoon and continue as above.

3. Spoon the batter into the prepared pan and bake in the oven for 1–1¼ hours, or until a toothpick inserted into the center comes out clean.

4. Let cool in the pan for 5 minutes, then turn out onto a wire rack to cool completely. Serve dusted with confectioners' sugar.

SPICED MARMALADE CAKE

SERVES 24

- ½ cup (1 stick) butter, plus extra for greasing
- ⅔ cup dark corn syrup
- ½ cup superfine sugar
- 2 tablespoons chunky marmalade
- 2 tablespoons finely chopped candied peel (optional)
- 2 cups self-rising flour
- 2 teaspoons apple pie spice
- 1 teaspoon ground ginger
- ½ teaspoon baking soda
- ⅔ cup milk
- 2 eggs, beaten

Topping
- 2 oranges, thinly sliced
- ¼ cup superfine sugar
- ¾ cup water
- 2 tablespoons marmalade

1. Preheat the oven to 350°F. Grease and line the bottom of a deep 8-inch square cake pan.

2. In a saucepan, gently heat the butter, corn syrup, sugar, and marmalade until they have melted. Remove from the heat and stir in the chopped peel, if using, and the dry ingredients. Then add the milk and beaten eggs and mix until smooth.

3. Pour the batter into the prepared pan and bake for 35–40 minutes, or until well risen and a toothpick inserted into the center comes out clean.

4. Meanwhile, make the topping. In a saucepan, combine the orange slices, sugar, and water and simmer, covered, for 25 minutes, or until tender. Remove the lid and cook for an additional 5 minutes, or until the liquid has been reduced to about 2 tablespoons. Add the marmalade and heat until it has melted.

5. Let the cake cool in the pan for 10 minutes, then turn out onto a wire rack and peel off the lining paper. Put on a serving plate and spoon the oranges and sauce over the top.

CHUNKY FRUIT & NUT CAKE

Because the ingredients for this cake are melted together in a saucepan, no creaming is involved, and the fruit plumps in the sweet, buttery juices.

SERVES 24

- 1¼ cups (2½ sticks) unsalted butter, plus extra for greasing
- 1⅔ cups light brown sugar
- 2½ pounds mixed dried fruit
- Finely grated zest and juice of 1 lemon
- ¾ cup plus 1 tablespoon sherry
- 4 tablespoons brandy
- 2 tablespoons apple pie spice
- ¾ cup Brazil nuts, roughly chopped
- ¾ cup hazelnuts, coarsely chopped
- 1⅓ cups ground hazelnuts
- 5 eggs, beaten
- 3 cups all-purpose flour

1. Slice the butter into a large, heavy-bottom saucepan and add the sugar, dried fruit, lemon zest and juice, sherry, brandy, and spice. Heat gently until the butter melts, stirring frequently. Gently simmer for about 10 minutes, or until the juices are thick and syrupy. Let cool for at least 30 minutes.

2. Meanwhile, preheat the oven to 275°F. Grease and line a 9-inch round or 8-inch square cake pan. Grease the paper.

3. Stir all the nuts and the eggs into the fruit mixture. Add the flour and mix until everything is evenly combined.

4. Turn the batter into the prepared pan and level the surface. Bake in the oven for 2¾–3 hours, or until a toothpick inserted into the center comes out clean.

5. Let cool in the pan, then remove and wrap in aluminum foil until needed.

TIP

- This is a superb cake to serve on its own or covered with marzipan and royal icing as a festive centerpiece. For extra flavor, prick the surface of the cake with a toothpick and spoon over 4–5 tablespoons brandy or sherry before storing.

RED FRUIT TEABREAD

Grinding your own almonds in a blender or food processor will always give the freshest, nuttiest flavor, as it does in this recipe. This fruity slice can be served plain or lightly buttered.

SERVES 8

- 7oz mixed dried red fruit, such as sour cherries, cranberries, and strawberries
- ⅔ cup hot fruit tea, such as raspberry, strawberry, or cranberry
- Butter, for greasing
- ⅔ cup whole blanched almonds
- ½ cup light brown sugar
- 1 egg, beaten
- ½ cup plus 1½ tablespoons self-rising flour
- ½ teaspoon baking powder
- Raw brown sugar, to serve

1. In a bowl, combine the dried fruit and fruit tea, cover, and let stand for 1 hour, or until most of the tea has been absorbed.

2. Preheat the oven to 350°F. Grease and line a 1-pound loaf pan. Grease the paper.

3. Coarsely chop half of the almonds, then grind the remainder in a food processor or blender. Stir the chopped and ground almonds, light brown sugar, egg, flour, and baking powder into the soaked fruit and stir until everything is combined.

4. Turn the batter into the prepared pan and level the surface. Bake in the oven for about 45 minutes, or until firm to the touch and a toothpick inserted into the center comes out clean. Transfer to a wire rack to cool and sprinkle with raw brown sugar.

STOLLEN

SERVES 12

- ⅔ cup golden raisins
- ⅓ cup finely chopped candied peel
- 4 tablespoons dark rum
- 2 teaspoons active dry yeast
- 4 tablespoons superfine sugar, plus 1 teaspoon
- ¾ cup plus 1 tablespoon lukewarm milk
- 2½ cups bread flour, plus extra if needed and for dusting
- Finely grated zest of 1 lemon
- ⅔ cup pistachios
- 4 tablespoons (½ stick) butter, melted
- Vegetable oil, for oiling
- 8 oz white marzipan, shaped into a 10-inch long sausage
- Confectioners' sugar, for dusting

1. In a bowl, combine the golden raisins, candied peel, and rum. Cover, and let soak for 1 hour.

2. Meanwhile, in a separate bowl, stir the yeast and the 1 teaspoon superfine sugar into the milk and let stand for 10 minutes, or until frothy.

3. In a large bowl, combine the flour, lemon zest, remaining superfine sugar, and pistachios. Add the melted butter and yeast mixture and, with a round-bladed knife, mix to a soft dough, adding a little more flour if it feels sticky.

4. Turn the dough onto a floured work surface and knead for 10 minutes, or until smooth and elastic. Place in a lightly oiled bowl, cover with plastic wrap, and let stand in a warm place for 1–2 hours, or until doubled in size.

5. Punch the dough down to deflate it, then knead in the fruit. Roll out to an oval about 12 x 7 inches and lay the marzipan slightly to one side of the center. Brush the long edges of the dough with water and fold the wider piece of dough over the filling, pressing down gently.

6. Transfer to an oiled baking sheet, cover with oiled plastic wrap, and let prove for 45 minutes, or until doubled in size.

7. Meanwhile, preheat the oven to 375°F. Remove the plastic wrap and bake in the oven for 30 minutes, or until golden. Transfer to a wire rack to cool. Serve generously dusted with confectioners' sugar.

FLORENTINE FRUIT CAKE

This cake is moist and semirich. It's topped with a delicious sugary crust of fruit and nuts that looks really stunning, especially when it's glistening with drizzled honey.

SERVES 12

- 1 cup plus 2 tablespoons (2¼ sticks) unsalted butter, softened, plus extra for greasing
- 1¼ cups superfine sugar
- 4 eggs, beaten
- 2 teaspoons vanilla extract
- 2¼ cups all-purpose flour, plus 2 tablespoons
- 1 tablespoon apple pie spice
- 1 cup plus 2 tablespoons slivered almonds
- 1 cup glacé cherries, halved
- 1 cup golden raisins
- 1 cup raisins
- 1 tablespoon heavy cream
- ⅓ cup whole blanched almonds
- Clear honey, to serve

1. Grease and line a 7-inch round or 6-inch square cake pan. Grease the paper. Preheat the oven to 300°F.

2. In a bowl, beat 1 cup of the butter with all except 2 tablespoons of the sugar until light and fluffy.

3. Gradually beat in the eggs, a little at a time, beating well after each addition. Stir in the vanilla extract. Sift in the 2¼ cups flour and spice and fold in with a large metal spoon. Add a generous half of the slivered almonds and the cherries and all of the golden raisins and raisins except 2 tablespoons of each. Mix until just combined.

4. Turn the batter into the prepared pan and level the surface.

5. In a small saucepan, gently heat the remaining butter until it melts, then stir in the remaining sugar. Add the 2 tablespoons flour, the cream, and the remaining fruit and nuts, including the whole almonds, then spread over the cake batter.

6. Bake in the oven for 1¾ hours, or until a toothpick inserted into the center comes out clean. Let cool in the pan. Serve drizzled with honey.

JAMAICAN RUM CAKE

The rum in this moist, fruity cake has a vibrant kick. Dark and spicy, it's a good cake for winter and can be served either plain as it is, or covered with marzipan and royal icing as a Christmas cake.

SERVES 12–16

- 4 cups mixed dried fruit
- ¾ cup glacé cherries, halved
- 1 cup dark rum
- 2 tablespoons blackstrap molasses
- ¾ cup (1½ sticks) unsalted butter, softened, plus extra for greasing
- ¾ cup plus 2 tablespoons dark brown sugar
- 4 eggs, beaten
- 1⅔ cups plus 1 tablespoon self-rising flour
- 2 tablespoons ground ginger

1. In a large bowl, combine the dried fruit and cherries, then pour in the rum. Stir well, cover, and let stand for 24 hours, stirring occasionally.

2. Preheat the oven to 300°F. Grease and line a 8-inch round or 7-inch square pan. Grease the paper.

3. Drain 2⅔ cups of the soaked fruit from the bowl with a slotted spoon and process in a food processor with the molasses until puréed.

4. In a large bowl, beat the butter and sugar together until pale and creamy. Gradually beat in the eggs, a little at a time, beating well after each addition and adding a little of the flour if the batter starts to curdle.

5. Stir in the remaining flour, the ginger, the remaining soaked fruit with any unabsorbed rum, and the fruit purée. Stir with a large metal spoon until well mixed.

6. Turn the batter into the prepared pan and level the surface. Bake in the oven for 2½–3 hours, or until firm and a toothpick inserted into the center comes out clean. Let cool in the pan.

CHRISTMAS FRUIT CAKE

SERVES 20-30

- 1⅔ cups golden raisins
- 1 cup plus 2 tablespoons raisins
- 1½ cups dried cranberries,
- 1¼ cups currants, chopped
- Grated zest and juice of 1 orange
- ¾ cup plus 1 tablespoon whiskey
- Vegetable oil, for oiling
- 1 cup plus 2 tablespoons (2¼ sticks) unsalted butter, softened
- 1¼ cups dark brown sugar
- 5 eggs
- 2 cups all-purpose flour
- 1 tablespoon baking powder
- 1½ tablespoons apple pie spice
- 1 cup glacé cherries, chopped
- ⅓ cup finely chopped mixed peel
- 1½ cups coarsely chopped Brazil nuts
- 1½ cups coarsely chopped blanched almonds
- ½ cup ground almonds
- 2 tablespoons thick-cut orange marmalade

1. In a large bowl, combine the golden raisins, raisins, cranberries, currants, and orange zest and juice, then pour in half of the whiskey. Stir well, cover, and let stand overnight.

2. Preheat the oven to 325°F. Oil and line a 10-inch round cake pan with 2 layers of parchment paper.

3. In a separate large bowl, beat the butter and sugar together until light and fluffy. Beat in the eggs, one at a time, beating well and adding 2 tablespoons of the flour after each addition.

4. Sift the remaining flour, baking powder, and spice together, then fold into the creamed mixture with a large metal spoon alternately with all the remaining ingredients except the remaining whiskey.

5. Transfer the batter to the prepared pan and level the surface, making a small dip in the center. Bake in the oven for 1 hour. Reduce the temperature to 300°F and bake for an additional 1¼-1½ hours, or until the cake is cooked and a toothpick inserted into the center comes out clean.

6. Prick the cake all over with a toothpick and pour over the reserved whiskey. Let cool in the pan for 30 minutes, then transfer to a wire rack to cool completely. Store, well wrapped in foil, for up to three months.

SIMNEL CAKE

A classic Easter simnel cake has a delicious layer of marzipan running through the center, which mingles with the flavors of the fruit cake.

SERVES 16-18

- ¾ cup (1½ sticks) unsalted butter, softened, plus extra for greasing
- ¾ cup plus 2 tablespoons superfine sugar
- 3 oz fresh ginger, grated
- 3 eggs, plus 1 egg white, lightly beaten
- 1¾ cups all-purpose flour
- 2 teaspoons apple pie spice
- 3⅓ cups mixed dried fruit
- 1 pound white marzipan
- Confectioners' sugar, for dusting
- Cape gooseberries, to decorate

1. Preheat the oven to 300°F. Grease and line a 7-inch round cake pan. Grease the paper.

2. In a large bowl, beat the butter, superfine sugar, and ginger together until light and fluffy. Beat in the whole eggs, one at a time, beating well after each addition and adding a little of the flour if the batter starts to curdle. Stir in the flour and spice, then the dried fruit.

3. Spoon half of the batter into the prepared pan and level the surface. Roll out half of the marzipan on a work surface dusted with confectioners' sugar to a circle slightly smaller than the pan. Lay over the batter and then cover with the remaining batter.

4. Bake in the oven for 2–2½ hours, or until a toothpick inserted into the center comes out clean. Let cool in the pan.

5. To decorate, brush the top with a little egg white. Roll out the remaining marzipan to a 7-inch circle and lay over the cake. Crimp the edge and brush with beaten egg white. Place under a hot broiler, watching closely, for 2 minutes, or until golden. Let cool, then decorate with Cape gooseberries dusted with confectioners' sugar.

FRUIT & NUT CUPCAKES

SERVES 18

- ½ cup plus 2 tablespoons (1¼ sticks) lightly salted butter, softened
- ¾ cup light brown sugar
- Scant 1⅔ cups self-rising flour
- 3 eggs
- 1 teaspoon almond extract
- ⅓ cup chopped mixed nuts
- Scant ⅓ cup mixed dried fruit

1. Preheat the oven to 350°F. Line two 12-section mini tart pans with 18 paper cake liners.

2. In a large bowl, beat the butter, sugar, flour, eggs, and almond extract together with an electric hand mixer for 1–2 minutes, or until light and creamy. Add the nuts and dried fruit and stir until evenly combined.

3. Divide the batter evenly among the cake liners and bake in the oven for 25 minutes, or until risen and just firm to the touch. Transfer to a wire rack to cool.

LEMON POLENTA CAKE & RED WINE STRAWBERRIES P59

SPECIAL OCCASIONS

APRICOT & ORANGE SWISS ROLL

SERVES 8

- 4 eggs
- ½ cup plus 2 tablespoons superfine sugar, plus extra for dusting
- Finely grated zest of 1 orange
- 1 cup all-purpose flour, sifted

Filling

- 1 cup ready-to-eat dried apricots
- ¾ cup plus 1 tablespoon apple juice

1. Make the filling. In a saucepan, simmer the apricots and apple juice, covered, for 10 minutes, or until most of the liquid has been absorbed. Purée in a blender or food processor, then let cool.

2. Preheat the oven to 400°F. Line a 12- x 9-inch roasting or jelly roll pan.

3. In a large heatproof bowl set over a saucepan of gently simmering water, whip the eggs, sugar, and orange zest together with an electric hand mixer until pale, creamy, and thick enough for the beaters to leave a trail when lifted from the bowl. Gently fold in the flour with a large metal spoon.

4. Pour the mixture into the prepared pan and gently spread into the corners. Bake in the oven for 8–10 minutes, or until golden brown and just beginning to shrink away from the sides, and the top springs back when gently pressed with a fingertip.

5. Meanwhile, sprinkle a sheet of parchment paper with a little sugar.

6. Quickly turn the cooked sponge out onto the sugared paper. Carefully peel off the lining paper. Spread with the apricot purée and roll up, starting from a short side and using the paper to help you. Let cool, seam-side down, on a wire rack. Serve the same day.

CRANBERRY & PEAR UPSIDE-DOWN CAKE

This is an ideal cake to make at Christmas, because it can be served warm with cream as a dessert, then cold the next day with coffee or tea.

SERVES 6-8

- Scant 1 cup fresh cranberries
- 2 tablespoons superfine sugar
- 1 large pear, peeled, cored, and sliced
- ¾ cup (1½ sticks) butter, softened, plus extra for greasing
- ¾ cup plus 2 tablespoons superfine sugar
- 3 eggs
- 1½ cups plus 1 tablespoon self-rising flour
- Finely grated zest of 1 orange
- 2 tablespoons orange juice

To serve
- Thick cranberry sauce
- Whipped cream
- Confectioners' sugar

1. Preheat the oven to 350°F. Grease and line the bottom of an 8-inch round springform cake pan.

2. Sprinkle the cranberries and superfine sugar over the bottom of the pan, then arrange the pear slices on top.

3. In a bowl, beat the butter and sugar together until light and fluffy. Gradually beat in the eggs and flour until smooth, then mix in the orange rind and juice.

4. Spoon the batter over the pears and level the surface. Bake in the oven for 1–1¼ hours, or until well risen and golden and a toothpick inserted into the center comes out clean. Check after 45 minutes and cover with foil if the cake appears to be browning too quickly.

5. Loosen the edge of the cake, cover it with a large plate, then invert the pan onto the plate and remove. While still hot, spoon a little cranberry sauce over the top. Serve warm or cold, cut into wedges with whipped cream and a dusting of confectioners' sugar.

TIP

- Frozen cranberries can be used instead of fresh, but be sure to thaw them thoroughly first.

PUMPKIN CAKE WITH VANILLA CARAMEL

This would make an ideal centerpiece at Thanksgiving. You can also use orange-fleshed winter squash in place of the pumpkin to vary the recipe.

SERVES 10
- ½ lb skinned and seeded pumpkin
- ¾ cup (1½ sticks) unsalted butter, softened, plus extra for greasing
- ¾ cup plus 2 tablespoons light brown sugar
- 1⅓ cups plus 1 tablespoon self-rising flour
- 1 teaspoon baking powder
- 2 teaspoons ground coriander
- 3 eggs
- ¾ cup ground almonds

Vanilla caramel
- ½ cup superfine sugar
- 4 tablespoons water
- 2 tablespoons light cream
- 2 teaspoons vanilla extract

1. Preheat the oven to 325°F. Grease and line an 8-inch round cake pan. Grease the paper. Finely grate the pumpkin and pat dry on kitchen paper.

2. In a bowl, beat the butter, sugar, flour, baking powder, coriander, eggs, and almonds together until smooth and creamy. Stir in the pumpkin.

3. Turn the batter into the prepared pan and level the surface. Bake in the oven for about 45 minutes, or until a toothpick inserted into the center comes out clean. Transfer to a wire rack to cool.

5. Make the vanilla caramel. In a small, heavy-bottom saucepan, gently heat the sugar and water, stirring, until the sugar dissolves. Bring to a boil and boil until the syrup turns to a golden caramel. Remove from the heat and stir in the cream and vanilla extract. Gently heat until smooth.

6. Transfer the cake to a serving plate and spoon over the caramel. Serve with extra caramel, if you like.

PLUM CRUMBLE CAKE WITH CINNAMON CREAM

SERVES 8-10

- ¾ cup butter (1½ sticks), softened, plus extra for greasing
- ¾ cup plus 2 tablespoons superfine sugar
- 3 eggs, lightly beaten
- 1¾ cups self-rising flour
- 1 teaspoon baking powder
- 1 cup ground almonds
- 6 ripe plums, halved and pitted

Crumble
- 3 tablespoons all-purpose flour
- ⅓ cup rolled oats
- 2 tablespoons (¼ stick) unsalted butter, finely diced
- 4 tablespoons light brown sugar
- Scant ⅔ cup coarsely chopped almonds

Cinnamon crème fraîche
- ¾ cup plus 1 tablespoon crème fraîche or equal quantities sour cream and whipping cream
- 1 tablespoon confectioners' sugar, sifted
- 1 teaspoon ground cinnamon

1. Preheat the oven 350°F. Grease and line the bottom of a 9½-inch cake pan.

2. Make the crumble. In a bowl, combine the flour and oats, then rub in the butter with the fingertips. Stir in the sugar and almonds. Set aside.

3. In a bowl, beat the butter and sugar together until light and fluffy. Gradually beat in the eggs, a little at a time, beating well after each addition. Sift in the flour and baking powder, add the ground almonds, and fold in with a large metal spoon until evenly combined.

4. Spoon the batter into the prepared pan and level the surface. Arrange the plums, cut-side up, over the top of the cake, pressing down gently into the batter. Scatter the crumble mixture evenly over the plums.

5. Bake in the oven for 50–60 minutes, or until the cake is risen and a toothpick inserted into the center comes out clean. Let cool in the pan for 15 minutes, then turn out onto a wire rack to cool completely.

6. Make the cinnamon crème fraîche. In a bowl, beat the ingredients together until smooth and chill until required. Serve the cake in wedges with the cinnamon crème fraîche.

LAVENDER MADEIRA CAKE

This is a buttery cake with a lovely, scented summer flavor. Make sure the lavender is fresh and that it has not been sprayed.

SERVES 8-10

- 3 sprigs of fresh lavender, each about 4 inches long
- ¾ cup (1½ sticks) unsalted butter, softened, plus extra for greasing
- ¾ cup superfine sugar
- Finely grated zest of 1 lemon
- 3 eggs, beaten
- 1¾ cups self-rising flour

Frosting
- 4 tablespoons milk
- 3 sprigs of fresh lavender, each about 4 inches long, plus extra small sprigs to decorate
- 1½ cups confectioners' sugar, sifted
- Lavender food coloring (optional)

1. Preheat the oven to 350°F. Grease and line a deep 8-inch round cake pan.

2. Remove the lavender flowers from the stalks, discarding the stalks. In a bowl, beat the butter and sugar together until light and fluffy. Add the lavender flowers, lemon zest, eggs, and flour and beat until smooth and creamy.

3. Turn the batter into the prepared pan and level the surface. Bake in the oven for 30 minutes, then reduce the oven temperature to 325°F and bake for an additional 15-25 minutes, or until a toothpick inserted into the center comes out clean. Let cool in the pan for 5 minutes, then turn out onto a wire rack to cool completely.

4. Meanwhile, make the frosting. In a very small saucepan, bring the milk and lavender sprigs just to a boil, then remove from the heat. Cover and let stand for about 20 minutes. Strain into a bowl and let cool completely.

5. In a separate bowl, mix just enough of the infused milk (1-2 tablespoons) into the confectioners' sugar to make a thick coating consistency. Add a few drops of food coloring, if you like. Spread the frosting evenly over the cake and decorate with small lavender sprigs. Serve in slices.

LEMON POLENTA CAKE & RED WINE STRAWBERRIES

Cornmeal (polenta) adds a lovely texture and nutty flavor to this cake. With its rich red wine and strawberry syrup, it is especially good when served as a dessert.

SERVES 8-10

- I cup all-purpose flour
- I½ teaspoons baking powder
- ¾ cup cornmeal (polenta)
- 3 eggs, plus 2 egg whites
- ¾ cup plus 2 tablespoons superfine sugar
- Finely grated zest and juice of 2 lemons
- 1/3 cup plus I tablespoon vegetable oil, plus extra for oiling
- 2/3 cup buttermilk

Red wine strawberries
- I¼ cups red wine
- I vanilla bean, split
- ¾ cup superfine sugar
- 2 tablespoons balsamic vinegar
- I¾ cups fresh strawberries, hulled

1. Preheat the oven to 350°F. Oil and line the bottom of a 10-inch round springform cake pan.

2. Sift the flour and baking powder into a bowl and stir in the cornmeal.

3. In a separate clean bowl, whip the eggs, egg whites, and sugar with an electric hand mixer for 3-4 minutes, or until pale and thickened. Stir in the cornmeal mixture, lemon zest and juice, oil, and buttermilk.

4. Pour the batter into the prepared pan and bake in the oven for 30 minutes, or until risen and firm to the touch. Let cool in the pan for 10 minutes, then turn out onto a wire rack to cool completely.

5. Prepare the red wine strawberries. In a saucepan, gently heat the wine, vanilla bean, and sugar until the sugar dissolves. Increase the heat and simmer for 10-15 minutes, or until reduced and syrupy. Let cool, then stir in the balsamic vinegar and strawberries. Cut the cake into slices and serve with the strawberries and their syrup.

APRICOT FRANGIPANE CAKE

This cake makes a fabulous gift when it's wrapped in ribbon-tied parchment paper. Cranberries are ideal for the festive season, but can be left out at other times of the year.

SERVES 8

- ¾ cup (1½ sticks) unsalted butter, softened, plus extra for greasing
- ¾ cup plus 2 tablespoons superfine sugar
- 3 eggs
- ¾ cup plus 1 tablespoon self-rising flour
- 1¾ cups ground almonds
- 1¼ cups ready-to-eat dried apricots
- 5 tablespoons smooth apricot jam
- 2 tablespoons brandy or almond liqueur
- 8 oz white almond paste
- ⅔ cup whole blanched almonds
- ¼ cup dried cranberries
- Glacé Icing (see page 150)

1. Preheat the oven to 325°F. Grease and line a 7-inch round cake pan. Grease the paper.

2. In a bowl, beat the butter, sugar, eggs, flour, and ground almonds until smooth and creamy. Coarsely chop the apricots and stir in 1½ cups.

3. Turn the batter into the prepared pan and level the surface. Bake in the oven for 50 minutes, or until just firm and a toothpick inserted into the center comes out clean. Transfer to a wire rack to cool.

4. Measure the circumference of the cake with a piece of string. In a small saucepan, gently heat the jam and liqueur until melted smooth. Brush a bit of the mixture over the top and side of the cake.

5. Roll out the almond paste and trim to a strip the length of the string and ½ inch deeper than the cake. Roll up the paste and unroll it around the side of the cake.

6. Scatter with the remaining apricots, and the nuts, and cranberries. Brush with the remaining glaze and scribble with glacé icing.

RASPBERRY & AMARETTI LAYER CAKE

Make the almondy sponge a day before assembling the cake if you can. This gives it time to firm up and makes slicing easier.

SERVES 10-12

- Butter, for greasing
- 4 oz amaretti cookies
- 5 eggs
- ½ cup superfine sugar
- 1 cup all-purpose flour
- ¾ cup Disaronno or other almond liqueur
- 2¼ cups mascarpone cheese
- Heaping ⅓ cup confectioners' sugar, plus extra for dusting
- 1¼ cups heavy cream
- 3¼ cups fresh raspberries

1. Preheat the oven to 350°F. Grease and line the bottoms of two 8-inch round shallow cake pans.

2. Place the cookies in a plastic bag and crush them with a rolling pin.

3. In a heatproof bowl set over a saucepan of gently simmering water, whip the eggs and superfine sugar together with an electric hand mixer until pale, creamy, and thick enough for the beaters to leave a trail when lifted from the bowl. Remove from the heat and beat for an additional 2 minutes. Sift in the flour and sprinkle with the cookie crumbs, then fold in with a large metal spoon.

4. Divide the batter evenly among the prepared pans and bake in the oven for 25 minutes, or until just firm. Transfer to a wire rack to cool.

5. Slice each cake horizontally in half and drizzle the layers with half of the liqueur. Whip the mascarpone with the remaining liqueur and confectioners' sugar until smooth. Add the cream and whip until peaking.

6. Reserve 1⅔ cups raspberries and lightly mash the remainder. Sandwich the cake layers together with the mashed raspberries and a little of the cream mixture. Spread the remainder over the top and side. Scatter with the reserved berries and serve dusted with confectioners' sugar.

CHILE & PINEAPPLE TORTE

This buttery sponge is specked with red chile and drizzled with vodka syrup after baking, giving a flavor that's far from predictable. A cake for adventurous cooks!

SERVES 8-10

- 1 large, medium-strength red chile, seeded and thinly sliced
- ¾ cup (1½ sticks) unsalted butter, softened, plus extra for greasing
- 1⅓ cups plus 1 tablespoon superfine sugar
- 3 eggs
- 2 cups plus 3 tablespoons self-rising flour
- 1 teaspoon baking powder
- 1¼ cups chopped dried pineapple
- ½ small fresh pineapple
- 4 tablespoons water
- 6 tablespoons vodka

1. Preheat the oven to 350°F. Grease and line a 9-inch round cake pan. Grease the paper.

2. In a bowl, beat half of the chile, the butter, ¾ cup plus 2 tablespoons of the sugar, the eggs, flour, and baking powder together until smooth and creamy. Stir in the dried pineapple.

3. Turn the batter into the prepared pan and level the surface. Cut away the skin and core from the fresh pineapple and thinly slice the flesh into rounds. Arrange over the batter with the remaining chile.

4. Bake in the oven for 1 hour, or until just firm and a toothpick inserted into the center comes out clean. Transfer to a wire rack.

5. Meanwhile, in a saucepan, gently heat the remaining sugar and water until the sugar dissolves. Bring to a boil and boil for 5 minutes, or until thickened and syrupy.

6. Pierce the warm cake all over with a toothpick and drizzle with half of the vodka. Stir the remaining vodka into the syrup and drizzle over the top.

MANGO & COCONUT CAKE

Use very ripe mangoes for this cake, to provide a sweet juicy contrast to the tangy lime syrup. Rum is a natural partner for lime, but vodka or tequila would work just as well.

SERVES 10-12

- 2 oz creamed coconut, chilled
- ⅔ cup (1 stick plus 2½ tablespoons) unsalted butter, softened, plus extra for greasing
- ¾ cup superfine sugar
- 1⅓ cups plus 1 tablespoon self-rising flour
- 1 teaspoon baking powder
- 3 eggs
- 1 teaspoon vanilla extract

To finish
- ⅓ cup plus 1 tablespoon superfine sugar
- ⅓ cup plus 1 tablespoon water
- Finely grated zest and juice of 3 limes
- 5 tablespoons white rum
- 1¼ cups extra-thick heavy cream
- 2 medium mangoes, pitted, peeled, and thinly sliced
- Confectioners' sugar, for dusting
- Toasted coconut shavings, to decorate

1. Preheat the oven to 350°F. Grease and line a 9-inch round cake pan. Grease the paper.

2. Finely grate the creamed coconut. In a bowl, beat the butter, sugar, flour, baking powder, eggs, and vanilla extract together until smooth and creamy. Stir in the coconut.

3. Turn the batter into the prepared pan and level the surface. Bake in the oven for 25–30 minutes, or until just firm. Transfer to a wire rack to cool.

4. To finish the cake, in a small saucepan, gently heat the sugar and water until the sugar dissolves. Heat for an additional 3 minutes, then let cool.

5. Slice the cake horizontally into 3 layers. Stir the lime zest and juice and rum into the syrup, then drizzle 3 tablespoonfuls over each cake.

6. In a bowl, whip the cream and the remaining syrup until the mixture holds its shape. Sandwich the cakes with the mango and flavored cream, dust the top with confectioners' sugar and decorate with coconut shavings.

COCONUT FROSTED ANGEL CAKE

Angel cake is just as good a way to use up leftover egg whites as a pavlova or meringue. This creamy white, airy sponge is smothered in a contrastingly rich coconut frosting.

SERVES 10-12

- Vegetable oil, for oiling
- 8 egg whites
- 1 teaspoon cream of tartar
- 1 cup plus 2 tablespoons superfine sugar
- 2 teaspoons vanilla extract
- 1 cup plus 3 tablespoons all-purpose flour, plus extra for dusting
- Coconut Frosting (see page 152)
- Toasted coconut shavings, to decorate

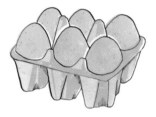

1. Preheat the oven to 325°F. Oil a 6¼-cup ring pan and lightly dust with flour, tapping out the excess.

2. In a large, thoroughly clean bowl, whip the egg whites with an electric hand mixer until frothy. Add the cream of tartar and whip until peaking. Gradually beat in the sugar, a tablespoonful at a time, beating well after each addition, until stiff and glossy. Beat in the vanilla extract with the last of the sugar. Sift in the flour and gently fold in with a large metal spoon.

3. Turn the batter into the prepared pan and level the surface. Bake in the oven for 25 minutes, or until firm to the touch and a toothpick inserted into the center comes out clean.

4. Invert the cake onto a wire rack but don't remove the pan. When cool, loosen the edges of the pan and turn the cake out onto a flat plate. Spread with coconut frosting and scatter the top with toasted coconut shavings to decorate.

ZUCCHINI & LIME CAKE

Zucchini, like some other vegetables, such as carrots, add a subtle flavor and moist texture to a simple sponge. Smother with glacé icing or cream cheese frosting, or leave plain.

SERVES 10

- 7½ oz zucchini
- 7 tablespoons (½ stick plus 3 tablespoons) unsalted butter, softened, plus extra greasing
- ½ cup superfine sugar
- Finely grated zest of 2 limes
- Scant ¼ cup honey
- 3 eggs
- 1¾ cups self-rising flour
- 1 teaspoon baking powder
- Heaping ⅓ hazelnuts, toasted and roughly chopped
- Glacé Icing (see page 150) or Cream Cheese Frosting (see page 151)

1. Preheat the oven to 325°F. Grease and line a 7-inch round cake pan. Grease the paper.

2. Coarsely grate the zucchini and pat between layers of paper towels to remove the excess moisture.

3. In a bowl, beat the butter, sugar, lime zest, honey, eggs, flour, and baking powder together until smooth and creamy. Stir in the grated zucchini and chopped hazelnuts.

4. Turn the batter into the prepared pan and level the surface. Bake in the oven for 1 hour, or until risen and golden and a toothpick inserted into the center comes out clean. Transfer to a wire rack to cool.

5. Place on a serving plate and drizzle the top with glacé icing or spread the top and side with the cream cheese frosting.

APPLE & CRANBERRY STREUSEL

There's only a tenuous link between this cake and a traditional German streusel, but it's easy to make and is no less tasty, especially served slightly warm with a spoonful of cream.

SERVES 6-8

- 2 cups self-rising flour
- ¾ cup (1½ sticks) unsalted butter, diced, plus extra for greasing
- ¾ cup plus 2 tablespoons superfine sugar, plus an extra 2 tablespoons
- 1 egg
- 4 tart apples, such as Granny Smith
- Scant ½ cup dried cranberries
- Confectioners' sugar, for dusting

1. Preheat the oven to 350°F. Grease a 7-inch round springform or loose-bottom cake pan.

2. In a food processor, process the flour and butter until the mixture resembles fine bread crumbs. Add the ¾ cup plus 2 tablespoons superfine sugar and process until the mixture just starts to make a coarse crumble.

3. Spoon out 6 oz of the mixture and add the egg to the remainder in the food processor. Process to a firm paste. Turn into the bottom of the prepared pan and press down gently in an even layer.

4. Peel, core, and slice the apples. Toss in a bowl with the cranberries and remaining superfine sugar. Scatter the fruit into the pan over the batter and sprinkle with the reserved crumble mix.

5. Bake in the oven for 50–60 minutes, or until deep golden. Let cool in the pan and serve lightly dusted with confectioners' sugar.

PEACH & RED CURRANT CREAM SPONGE

Whipped sponges have an incredibly light and airy texture, but this will last for only a day. However, you can add butter to make a Genoese sponge (see Tip), which you can store for longer.

SERVES 8-10

- Butter, for greasing
- ½ cup superfine sugar
- 4 eggs
- ¾ cup plus 1 tablespoon all-purpose flour

Filling
- 3½ oz fresh red currant sprigs
- ⅔ cup heavy or whipping cream
- 1 tablespoon superfine sugar, plus extra for dusting
- 1 ripe, juicy peach, pitted and sliced

1. Preheat the oven to 375°F. Grease and line the bottoms of two 8-inch round shallow cake pans.

2. In a large heatproof bowl set over a saucepan of gently simmering water, whip the sugar and eggs together with an electric hand mixer until pale, creamy, and thick enough for the beaters to leave a trail when lifted from the bowl. Remove from the heat and beat for an additional 2 minutes.

3. Sift in half of the flour and fold in with a large metal spoon. Sift and fold in the remaining flour. Divide the batter evenly among the prepared pans and spread gently to the edges. Bake in the oven for 20–25 minutes, or until just firm to the touch. Transfer to a wire rack to cool.

4. Make the filling. Reserve a few red currant sprigs. Remove the fruits of the remainder. In a bowl, whip the cream and sugar together and spread over one cake layer. Arrange the currants and peach slices on the surface and place the second cake on top. Decorate with the reserved currant sprigs and lightly dust with sugar.

TIP

- For a Genoese sponge, melt 4 tablespoons (½ stick) unsalted butter and let cool. Pour in half after sifting in the first addition of flour, then fold in with the flour. Add the remaining butter with the second addition of flour.

LIQUEUR-DRIZZLED COFFEE CAKE P90

CHOCOLATE & COFFEE

CHOCOLATE GUINNESS CAKE

SERVES 10

- ½ cup butter (1 stick), softened, plus extra for greasing
- 1 cup light brown sugar
- 1½ cups all-purpose flour
- ½ cup unsweetened cocoa, plus extra for dusting
- ½ teaspoon baking powder
- 1 teaspoon baking soda
- 3 eggs, beaten
- ¾ cup Guinness or other stout
- White chocolate curls, to decorate

White chocolate ganache
- ¾ cup heavy cream
- 7 oz white chocolate, broken into pieces

1. Preheat the oven to 325°F. Grease and line the bottom of an 8-inch round springform cake pan. Grease the paper.

2. In a bowl, beat the butter and sugar together until light and fluffy. Into another bowl, sift the flour, cocoa, baking powder, and baking soda. Into the butter mixture, gradually beat alternate spoonfuls of the egg, flour mixture, and the Guinness until all has been incorporated and the batter is smooth.

3. Spoon into the prepared pan and level the surface. Bake in the oven for 45–55 minutes, or until well risen, the top is slightly cracked, and a toothpick inserted into the center comes out clean. Let cool in the pan for 10 minutes, then turn out onto a wire rack and peel off the lining paper.

4. Make the white chocolate frosting. In a small saucepan, bring half of the cream just to a boil, then remove from the heat. Add the chocolate and let stand for 10 minutes until it melts. Stir, then chill for 15 minutes.

5. In a bowl, whip the remaining cream, then beat in the chocolate cream until thick. Chill for an additional 15 minutes.

6. Transfer the cake to a serving plate and spoon the frosting over the top. Decorate with white chocolate curls and dust with sifted cocoa.

DEVIL'S FOOD CAKE

SERVES 12

- 3 oz dark chocolate, broken into pieces
- ¾ cup strong black coffee
- ¾ cup (1½ sticks) unsalted butter, softened, plus extra, melted, for greasing
- 1¼ cups dark brown sugar
- ¼ cup vanilla sugar
- 3 eggs
- 2⅓ cups plus 1 tablespoon all-purpose flour, plus extra for dusting
- 1½ teaspoons baking soda
- ¾ cup sour cream

Frosting
- 2½ cups superfine or granulated sugar
- 1¼ cups water
- 2 egg whites, stiffly whipped

1. In a saucepan, gently heat the chocolate with the coffee, stirring, until it melts and the mixture is smooth. Let cool. Preheat the oven to 375°F. Grease and line three 8-inch round shallow cake pans. Brush the paper with melted butter and lightly dust with flour, tapping out the excess.

2. In a bowl, beat the butter and sugars together until light and fluffy. Add the eggs, one at a time, beating well after each addition. Stir in the chocolate mixture.

3. Sift the flour and baking soda onto a sheet of parchment paper and then gently fold in one-third of the flour mixture, then one-third of the sour cream into the creamed mixture. Repeat until all has been incorporated.

4. Divide the batter evenly among the prepared pans and bake in the oven for 25 minutes, or until a toothpick inserted into the center comes out clean. Let cool in the pans on a wire rack for 5 minutes, then turn out and let cool completely.

5. Make the frosting. In a heavy-bottom saucepan, gently heat the sugar and water, stirring, until the sugar dissolves. Increase the heat and bring to a boil. Simmer until the mixture reaches the soft ball stage: a bit placed in a glass of ice water should form soft, sticky balls. Remove from the heat and dip the pan bottom in cold water. Gradually beat the syrup into the whipped egg whites. Continue beating until the frosting thickens and loses its sheen. Quickly spread between the cake layers and over the top and side.

CHOCOLATE & RUM CAKE

SERVES 16

- 5 oz dark chocolate, broken into pieces
- Finely grated zest and juice of 1 orange
- Few drops rum extract (optional)
- ⅔ cup (1 stick plus 2½ tablespoons) unsalted butter, softened, plus extra for greasing
- ⅔ cup superfine sugar

- 4 eggs, separated
- 1¼ cups ground almonds
- 8–16 candied violet petals, to decorate (optional)

Chocolate frosting
- 5 oz dark chocolate, broken into pieces
- ½ cup (1 stick) unsalted butter

1. Preheat the oven to 350°F. Grease and line the bottoms of two 8-inch round shallow cake pans.

2. In a heatproof bowl set over a saucepan of gently simmering water, melt the chocolate with the orange zest and juice and rum extract, if using.

3. In a large bowl, beat the butter and all except 1 tablespoon of the sugar together until pale and creamy. Beat in the egg yolks, one at a time, beating well after each addition, then stir in the chocolate mixture.

4. In a separate large, thoroughly clean bowl, whip the egg whites with an electric hand mixer until softly peaking. Add the remaining sugar and beat until stiff. Fold the whipped egg whites into the chocolate mixture with the ground almonds, then spoon evenly into the prepared pans.

5. Bake in the oven for 20–25 minutes, or until the sides of the cakes are cooked but the centers are still a little unset. Let cool in the pans for a few minutes, then gently turn out onto a wire rack to cool completely.

6. Make the frosting. Melt the chocolate as before, then beat in the butter, a tablespoon at a time, until it melts. Remove from the heat and beat occasionally until cool. If the frosting is runny, chill to firm up. Sandwich the cakes with some of the frosting, then spread the remaining frosting evenly over the top and side. Decorate with candied violet petals, if you like.

CHOCOLATE & SWEET POTATO TORTE

SERVES 12-14

- 1¾ cups self-rising flour
- ½ cup unsweetened cocoa
- 1 teaspoon baking soda
- ¾ cup (1½ sticks) butter, softened, plus extra for greasing
- ¾ cup light brown sugar
- 3 eggs, beaten
- 13 oz sweet potato, boiled, drained, and mashed with 3 tablespoons milk
- ¼ cup chopped candied ginger, plus 3 tablespoons to decorate
- Candied rose petals or violets, to decorate

Frosting
- 5 oz dark chocolate
- 2 tablespoons light brown sugar
- ¾ cup sour cream

1. Preheat the oven to 325°F. Grease and line the bottom of a 9-inch round springform cake pan. Grease the paper.

2. In a bowl, combine the flour, cocoa, and baking soda. In a separate bowl, beat the butter and sugar together until pale and creamy. Gradually beat in alternate spoonfuls of the egg and flour mixture until all has been incorporated and the batter is smooth. Stir in the sweet potato and ginger.

3. Pour the batter into the prepared pan and level the surface. Bake in the oven for 45–50 minutes, or until the cake has risen with a slightly domed and cracked top and a toothpick inserted into the center comes out clean. Let cool in the pan for 15 minutes (don't worry if it sinks slightly), then turn out onto a wire rack and peel off the lining paper. Let cool completely.

4. Make the frosting. In a heatproof bowl placed over a saucepan of gently simmering water, melt the chocolate and sugar. Remove from the heat, add the sour cream, and stir until smooth and glossy. Chill for 10–30 minutes, or until the frosting is thick enough to spread.

5. Spoon the frosting over the top and side of the cake and swirl with a knife. Sprinkle with the ginger, and candied flower petals if you like, then let stand in a cool place to set.

CHOCOLATE MARBLE CAKE

You can use either a plain ring pan for this cake, or the more decorative kugelhopf or bundt pan if you prefer.

SERVES 8

- Vegetable oil, for oiling
- 1 cup plus 2 tablespoons (2¼ sticks) unsalted butter, softened
- ¾ cup plus 2 tablespoons superfine sugar
- 4 eggs, lightly beaten
- 1¾ cups self-rising flour
- 1 teaspoon baking powder
- Pinch of salt
- ½ cup ground almonds
- 4 oz dark chocolate
- 4 oz white chocolate

1. Preheat the oven to 350°F. Oil a 9-inch kugelhopf pan.

2. In a stand mixer, beat the butter, sugar, eggs, flour, baking powder, salt, and ground almonds together until evenly combined. Spoon half of the mixture into a clean bowl.

3. Meanwhile, place the dark and white chocolate in separate heatproof bowls and set each one over a saucepan of gently simmering water. Stir until the chocolate melts.

4. Reserving 2 tablespoons of each melted chocolate for decoration, stir the remaining dark chocolate into half of the cake batter and the remaining white chocolate into the remaining cake batter, folding together until evenly combined.

5. Spoon both batters alternately into the prepared pan and use a toothpick to swirl gently to create a marbled effect. Bake in the oven for 45–50 minutes, or until a toothpick inserted into the center comes out clean. Cover with foil if it browns too quickly. Let cool in the pan for 10 minutes, then turn out onto a wire rack to cool.

6. Immerse the bowls of the reserved chocolates in hot water, stirring until melted. Use teaspoons to drizzle over the cake and serve in slices.

CHOCOLATE PEANUT BUTTER CAKE

SERVES 20

- 1 cup (2 sticks) unsalted butter, softened, plus extra for greasing
- 2 cups light brown sugar
- ½ cup chunky peanut butter
- 4 oz dark chocolate, melted
- 1¾ cups all-purpose flour
- 2 teaspoons baking powder
- ½ teaspoon baking soda
- 4 eggs, beaten
- 5 tablespoons milk

Glaze & decoration
- 2 tablespoons (¼ stick) butter
- 2 tablespoons smooth peanut butter
- 3 tablespoons light corn syrup
- 1 teaspoon vanilla extract
- 1 cup dark chocolate chips
- ¼ cup confectioners' sugar
- Chocolate-coated peanuts (optional)

1. Preheat the oven to 350°F. Grease and line the bottom of a 10-inch round cake pan.

2. In a bowl, beat the butter and sugar together until light and fluffy. Beat in the peanut butter and melted chocolate. Sift the flour, baking powder, and baking soda into a separate bowl. Gradually beat the eggs into the creamed mixture, a little at a time, beating well after each addition and adding a little of the flour mixture if the batter starts to curdle. Fold in the remaining flour mixture and milk, mixing well.

3. Turn the batter into the prepared pan and level the surface. Bake in the oven for 50 minutes, or until a toothpick inserted into the center comes out clean. Let cool in the pan for a few minutes, then turn out onto a wire rack to cool completely.

4. Make the glaze. In a saucepan, gently heat the butter, peanut butter, corn syrup, and vanilla extract, stirring until the butter melts. Add the chocolate chips and stir until completely melted and smooth. Stir in the sugar. Remove from the heat and let cool until a thick pouring consistency.

5. Pour the glaze evenly over the cake and decorate with chocolate-coated peanuts if you like. Serve in slices.

PEPPERMINT-CHOCOLATE CAKE

SERVES 10-20

- 7 oz bittersweet chocolate, broken into squares
- 5 tablespoons (½ stick plus 1 tablespoon) unsalted butter, plus extra for greasing
- 2½ cups superfine sugar
- 3 egg yolks
- 1½ cups milk
- 2 cups self-rising flour
- Pinch of salt
- ¼ teaspoon baking soda
- 2 teaspoons vanilla extract

Frosting
- 3 egg whites
- 2 cups superfine sugar
- Pinch of salt
- ¼ teaspoon cream of tartar
- 3 tablespoons water
- 2-3 drops green food coloring
- 2-3 drops peppermint extract
- ¼ cup crushed peppermint candies

1. Preheat the oven to 350°F. Grease and line the bottoms of two 8-inch round shallow cake pans.

2. In a large heatproof bowl set over a saucepan of gently simmering water, melt the chocolate and butter, then let cool to room temperature. Stir in the sugar, then add the egg yolks and half of the milk and mix well.

3. Add the flour, salt, and baking soda and beat for 1 minute with an electric hand mixer. Beat in the remaining milk and vanilla extract.

4. Divide the batter evenly among the prepared pans and level the surface. Bake in the oven for 25-30 minutes, or until just firm to the touch. Turn out onto a wire rack and let cool.

5. Make the frosting. In a heatproof bowl set over a saucepan of gently simmering water, whip the egg whites, sugar, salt, cream of tartar, and water with the cleaned hand mixer for about 7 minutes, or until forming firm peaks. Remove from the heat and stir in the food coloring and peppermint extract. Sandwich the cakes with some of the frosting, then spread the remaining frosting evenly over the top and side. Decorate with the crushed sweets.

CHOCOLATE TRUFFLE CAKE

SERVES 8

- Vegetable oil, for oiling
- 8 oz dark chocolate, broken into pieces
- ½ cup (1 stick) unsalted butter
- 3 tablespoons heavy cream
- 4 eggs, separated
- ½ cup superfine sugar
- 2 tablespoons unsweetened cocoa, sifted, plus extra for dusting

To serve
- Whipped cream
- Fresh strawberries

1. Preheat the oven to 350°F. Oil and line the bottom of a 9-inch round springform cake pan, then lightly dust with cocoa, tapping out the excess.

2. In a heatproof bowl set over a saucepan of gently simmering water, melt the chocolate and butter with the cream. Remove from the heat and let cool for 5 minutes.

3. In a separate bowl, beat the egg yolks with three-quarters of the superfine sugar until pale, then stir in the cooled chocolate mixture.

4. In a large, thoroughly clean bowl, beat the egg whites with an electric hand mixer until forming soft peaks, then beat in the remaining superfine sugar. Fold into the egg yolk mixture with the cocoa until evenly mixed.

5. Pour the batter into the prepared pan and bake in the oven for 35 minutes.

6. Let cool in the pan for 10 minutes, then turn out onto a serving plate. Serve in wedges while still warm with whipped cream and strawberries.

WHITE & DARK TRUFFLE CAKE

SERVES 8-10

- Butter, for greasing
- 2 eggs
- ¼ cup superfine sugar
- 3 tablespoons cornstarch
- 2 tablespoons unsweetened cocoa
- 2 tablespoons cold strong black coffee
- 1 tablespoon whiskey
- Candied rose petals, to decorate

Dark layers
- 13 oz dark chocolate
- 2 cups heavy cream

White layer
- 7 oz white chocolate
- 1¼ cups heavy cream

1. Preheat the oven to 375°F. Grease and line the bottom of a 9-inch round springform cake pan. Grease the paper. In a large heatproof bowl set over a saucepan of gently simmering water, whip the eggs and sugar together with an electric hand mixer until pale, creamy, and thick enough for the beaters to leave a trail when lifted from the bowl. Remove from the heat.

2. Sift the cornstarch and cocoa three times into a bowl. Fold into the egg mixture until no streaks remain. Turn the batter into the prepared pan and level the surface. Bake in the oven for 7 minutes, or until risen. Let cool in the pan for 10 minutes, then turn out onto a wire rack, peel off the lining paper, and cool completely.

3. Wash and thoroughly dry the pan, then carefully return the cake. Combine the coffee and whiskey and brush or drizzle over the cake.

4. Make the first dark layer. In a heatproof bowl set over a saucepan of gently simmering water, melt half of the dark chocolate and let cool. Beat half of the cream until thick, then fold in the melted chocolate until smooth. Spread over the cake; bang the pan on the work surface once or twice to remove any air bubbles. Cover and chill.

5. Make the white layer in the same way and spread over the dark layer; bang the pan as before. Cover and chill, then make and spread a second dark layer in the same way. Smooth the surface, cover, and chill until set. To serve, remove the pan side and sprinkle with candied rose petals.

CHOCOLATE REFRIGERATOR CAKE

Refrigerator cakes are always a great favorite with adults and kids alike. This one is simple and quick to make, and you can substitute the raisins and cherries for fruits that you prefer, if you like.

SERVES 12-14

- I pound bittersweet chocolate, broken into squares
- 1¼ cups (2½ sticks) unsalted butter, plus extra for greasing
- 12 oz shortbread cookies or graham crackers, coarsely chopped
- 2 cups pecans, chopped
- I cup raisins
- I cup candied cherries, halved
- I handful mini marshmallows

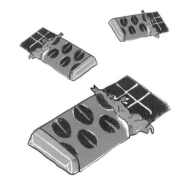

1. Grease and line a 10-inch loaf pan with a double layer of plastic wrap.

2. In a large heatproof bowl set over a saucepan of gently simmering water, melt the chocolate and butter. Remove from the heat, add all the remaining ingredients, and stir until well mixed.

3. Spoon the mixture into the prepared pan and level the surface. Cover and chill for 2-3 hours, or until firm enough to turn out. Serve in slices.

COFFEE, MAPLE & PECAN SPONGE CAKE

SERVES 6-8

- ½ cup all-purpose flour
- Pinch of salt
- 3 large eggs
- 6 tablespoons superfine sugar
- 1 teaspoon instant coffee powder dissolved in 1 tablespoon hot water
- ½ teaspoon vanilla extract
- 3 tablespoons (¼ stick plus 1 tablespoon) unsalted butter, melted, plus extra for greasing
- 8 pecan halves, to decorate

Frosting
- ¾ cup (1½ sticks) butter, softened
- Scant 1 cup confectioners' sugar
- 1 teaspoon instant coffee powder dissolved in 1 tablespoon hot water
- 4 tablespoons maple syrup

1. Preheat the oven to 350°F. Grease and line a deep 8-inch round cake pan.

2. Sift the flour and salt together three times into a bowl.

3. In a large heatproof bowl set over a saucepan of gently simmering water, whip the eggs and sugar together with an electric hand mixer until pale, creamy, and thick enough for the beaters to leave a trail when lifted from the bowl.

4. Beat in the coffee and vanilla extract. Sift in the flour mixture in three additions, drizzling a little of the melted butter around the edge of the batter after each addition, and carefully fold in with a large metal spoon.

5. Pour the batter evenly into the prepared pan and bake in the oven for 25–30 minutes, or until risen and golden. Let cool in the pan for 2–3 minutes, then turn out onto a wire rack to cool completely.

6. Make the frosting. In a bowl, beat the butter and sugar together until smooth, then gradually beat in the coffee and maple syrup.

7. Slice the cake horizontally into three layers. Sandwich the layers together with some of the frosting, then spread the remainder over the top and side. Decorate the top with the pecan halves.

COFFEE & WALNUT CAKE

Some classic cake recipes never lose their appeal, and this is certainly one of them. The cake itself is light and airy, and better for slicing if made a day in advance.

SERVES 10

- ¾ cup (1½ sticks) unsalted butter, softened, plus extra for greasing
- ¾ cup plus 2 tablespoons light brown sugar
- 3 eggs
- 1⅓ cups plus 1 tablespoon self-rising flour
- 1 teaspoon baking powder
- 1 tablespoon instant espresso powder dissolved in 2 tablespoons hot water
- Scant ½ cup chopped walnuts, plus extra halves to decorate
- Coffee Buttercream (see page 150)

1. Preheat the oven to 350°F. Grease and line the bottoms of two shallow 7-inch cake pans.

2. In a bowl, beat the butter, sugar, eggs, flour, and baking powder together until smooth and creamy. Beat in the coffee and chopped walnuts.

3. Divide the batter evenly among the prepared pans and level the surface. Bake in the oven for about 25 minutes, or until risen and just firm to the touch. Transfer to a wire rack to cool.

4. Sandwich the cakes together with half of the buttercream and spread the top of the cake with the remainder. Decorate with walnut halves.

COFFEE CAKE WITH PISTACHIO PRALINE

SERVES 12

- Vegetable oil, for oiling
- 6 eggs
- ¾ cup superfine sugar
- 1½ cups all-purpose flour, sifted
- 4 tablespoons (½ stick) unsalted butter, melted
- 2 tablespoons prepared espresso coffee, cooled
- ⅔ cup shelled pistachios
- ½ cup granulated sugar
- 3 tablespoons water

Maple syrup frosting
- 6 egg yolks
- ¾ cup superfine sugar
- ⅔ cup milk
- 1½ cups (3 sticks) unsalted butter, softened, diced
- 3 tablespoons maple syrup

1. Preheat the oven to 350°F. Oil and line the bottom of a 9-inch cake pan.

2. In a large heatproof bowl set over a saucepan of gently simmering water, whip the eggs and superfine sugar with an electric hand mixer until pale, creamy, and thick enough for the beaters to leave a trail when lifted from the bowl. Remove from the heat and fold in the flour, butter, and coffee.

3. Transfer the batter to the prepared pan and bake in the oven for 25–30 minutes. Let cool in the pan for 5 minutes, then turn out onto a wire rack to cool completely. Slice the cake horizontally into three layers.

4. Make the praline. Spread the pistachios on a baking sheet. In a heavy-bottom saucepan, heat the granulated sugar and water until the sugar dissolves. Increase the heat until the sugar turns light golden. Pour over the nuts and let set. Break the praline into pieces, then grind to a rough powder.

5. Make the frosting. In a bowl, beat the egg yolks and sugar together until pale. Heat the milk until just boiling, then beat into the egg mixture. Return to the pan and heat gently, stirring, until the mixture coats the back of the spoon. Remove from the heat and beat for 2–3 minutes, then gradually beat in the butter, a little at a time, until thick and glossy. Beat in the maple syrup.

6. Fold half of the praline into half of the frosting and use to sandwich the layers together. Spread the remainder over the top and side of the cake. Sprinkle with the remaining praline.

OLD-FASHIONED COFFEE CAKE

SERVES 8
- ¾ cup soft margarine, plus extra for greasing
- ¾ cup light brown or superfine sugar
- 1½ cups self-rising flour
- 1 teaspoon baking powder
- 3 eggs
- 3 teaspoons instant coffee dissolved in 2 teaspoons hot water
- 2 oz dark chocolate, melted

Frosting
- ⅓ cup (½ stick plus 1⅓ tablespoons) butter, softened
- 1⅓ cups confectioners' sugar, sifted
- 3 teaspoons instant coffee dissolved in 2 teaspoons hot water

1. Preheat the oven to 350°F. Grease and line the bottoms of two shallow 7-inch round cake pans.

2. In a large bowl or food processor, beat all the cake ingredients together until smooth. Divide the batter evenly among the prepared pans and level the surface. Bake in the oven for 20 minutes, or until well risen, browned, and springy to the touch. Let cool in the pans for a few minutes, then turn out onto a wire rack, peel off the lining paper, and let cool completely.

3. Make the frosting. In a bowl, beat the butter and half of the sugar together, then add the coffee and beat until smooth. Gradually beat in the remaining sugar until pale and creamy.

4. Place one of the cakes on a serving plate, spread with half of the frosting, then cover with the second cake. Spread the remaining frosting over the top. Pipe or drizzle swirls of the melted chocolate on top.

CAPPUCCINO TRUFFLE CAKE

This delicious coffee-and-chocolate combination is more like a cold soufflé than a cake. Serve with whipped cream, if you like.

SERVES 6-8

- 1 tablespoon instant coffee powder dissolved in a scant ⅔ cup hot water
- ½ cup pitted prunes, chopped
- 4 tablespoons Tia Maria or other coffee liqueur
- 6 oz bittersweet chocolate, broken into squares
- ½ cup (1 stick) unsalted butter, plus extra for greasing
- 5 eggs, separated
- ½ cup superfine sugar
- 1 teaspoon vanilla extract
- 1 tablespoon cornstarch
- Unsweetened cocoa, sifted, for dusting

1. In a small bowl, combine the hot coffee and prunes, then stir in the liqueur. Cover and let soak overnight.

2. Preheat the oven to 325°F. Grease and line an 8-inch round springform cake pan.

3. In a heatproof bowl set over a saucepan of gently simmering water, melt the chocolate and butter. Remove from the heat.

4. In a separate large heatproof bowl set over a saucepan of gently simmering water, whip the egg yolks and sugar together with an electric hand mixer until pale, creamy and thick enough for the beaters to leave a trail when lifted from the bowl. Remove from the heat.

5. Drain any excess liquid from the prunes and discard. Stir the vanilla extract, drained prunes, and melted chocolate into the creamy mixture.

6. In a large, thoroughly clean bowl, whip the egg whites with the cleaned hand mixer until stiff. Beat in the cornstarch, then fold into the chocolate mixture with a large metal spoon.

7. Pour the batter into the prepared pan and level the surface. Bake in the oven for 50 minutes, or until springy to the touch. Let cool completely in the pan. Turn the cake out onto a serving plate and dust with cocoa.

LIQUEUR-DRIZZLED COFFEE CAKE

For best results, use percolator coffee for this cake, with its stunning bands of coffee-and-almond flavoring. If you are using instant coffee, reduce the amount to 4 teaspoons.

SERVES 8

- 2 tablespoons espresso coffee powder
- ½ cup ground almonds
- ¼ cup dark brown sugar
- ¾ cup superfine sugar, plus 1 tablespoon
- ¾ cup (1½ sticks) unsalted butter, softened, plus extra for greasing
- 3 eggs
- 1½ cups plus 1 tablespoon self-rising flour
- 1 teaspoon baking powder
- ½ cup slivered almonds
- ½ teaspoon ground cinnamon
- 4 tablespoons coffee liqueur

1. Preheat the oven to 350°F. Grease and line a 7-inch round springform or loose-bottom cake pan. Grease the paper.

2. In a small bowl, combine the coffee powder, ground almonds, and brown sugar.

3. In a separate bowl, beat the ¾ cup superfine sugar, butter, eggs, flour, and baking powder together until smooth and creamy. Spread one-third of the sponge batter in the prepared pan and scatter with half of the coffee mixture. Gently spread with half of the remaining batter and scatter with the remaining coffee mixture. Finally, spread with the batter.

4. Toss the remaining tablespoon superfine sugar with the slivered almonds and cinnamon and scatter over the surface. Bake in the oven for 45 minutes, or until just firm and a toothpick inserted into the center comes out clean. Let cool in the pan for 10 minutes, then peel off the lining paper and transfer to a wire rack to cool completely. Drizzle with the coffee liqueur before serving.

RASPBERRY & COCONUT FRIANDS P104

SMALL CAKES

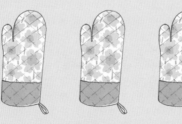

MINI CAPPUCCINO CAKES

SERVES 12

- ¾ cup (1½ sticks) lightly salted butter, softened, plus extra for greasing
- ¾ cup light brown sugar
- 1½ cups self-rising flour
- 2 tablespoons unsweetened cocoa
- ½ teaspoon baking powder
- 3 eggs
- 3 teaspoons instant coffee granules dissolved in 2 teaspoons hot water

To decorate

- 1¼ cups heavy cream
- 3 oz dark, bittersweet, or white chocolate curls

1. Preheat the oven to 350°F. Grease the sections of a 12-hole deep muffin pan and line the bottoms with circles of parchment paper.

2. In a bowl, beat all the cake ingredients except the coffee together with an electric hand mixer until smooth. Stir in the coffee.

3. Divide the batter evenly among the pan sections and level the surface. Bake in the oven for 12–14 minutes, or until well risen and just firm. Let cool in the pan for 5 minutes, then transfer to a wire rack to cool completely.

4. Slice each cake horizontally in half. In a bowl, whip the cream until softly peaking, then use to sandwich the cakes together in pairs and spoon the remainder on the tops. Sprinkle with the chocolate curls.

TIP

- These cakes are best eaten on the day they are made.

PEANUT CARAMEL CUPCAKES

- - - - - - - - - - - - - - -

SERVES 16

- 4 tablespoons (½ stick) lightly salted butter, softened
- ¼ cup light brown sugar
- ½ cup self-rising flour
- 1 egg
- ⅓ cup salted peanuts, finely chopped, plus extra to decorate

Frosting
- 4 tablespoons (½ stick) lightly salted butter
- ½ cup light brown sugar
- 3 tablespoons milk
- ¾ cup confectioners' sugar

1. Preheat the oven to 350°F. Place 16 mini silicone muffin cups on a baking sheet.

2. In a bowl, beat the butter, sugar, flour, and egg together with an electric hand mixer until pale and creamy. Stir in the chopped peanuts.

3. Divide the batter evenly among the muffin cups and bake in the oven for 10–12 minutes, or until risen and just firm. Let cool in the cups for 2 minutes, then transfer to a wire rack to cool completely.

4. Make the frosting. In a saucepan, gently heat the butter, brown sugar, and milk until the sugar dissolves. Bring to a boil and boil for 1 minute, or until the mixture turns slightly syrupy. Remove from the heat and pour into a bowl. Sift in the confectioners' sugar and beat until the mixture is smooth and fudge-like.

5. Spread the frosting over the tops of the cakes with a palette knife and sprinkle with chopped peanuts to decorate.

RED VELVET MINI CAKES

SERVES 16
- 1 cup self-rising flour
- 2 teaspoons unsweetened cocoa
- ¼ cup superfine sugar
- 1 small raw beet, coarsely grated
- 2 tablespoons vegetable oil
- 1 egg
- 3 tablespoons buttermilk
- 1 teaspoon white distilled or cider vinegar

Frosting
- 6 tablespoons cream cheese
- 4 tablespoons (½ stick) unsalted butter, softened
- 1 teaspoon vanilla bean paste
- 1 cup confectioners' sugar, sifted
- Small candied rose petals, to decorate

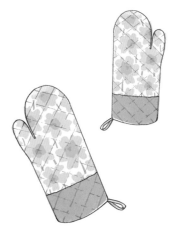

1. Preheat the oven to 350°F. Place 16 mini silicone muffin cups on a baking sheet.

2. Sift the flour and cocoa into a bowl. Stir in the sugar.

3. In a food processor or blender, process the beet, oil, and egg to make a smooth purée. Briefly blend in the buttermilk and vinegar. Add to the dry ingredients and mix until combined.

4. Divide the batter evenly among the muffin cups and bake in the oven for 10 minutes, or until risen and just firm. Let cool in the cups for 2 minutes, then transfer to a wire rack to cool completely.

5. Make the frosting. In a bowl, beat all the frosting ingredients together until smooth and creamy. Place in a pastry bag fitted with a small star trip and pipe swirls on top of the cakes. Decorate each with a rose petal.

STICKY TOFFEE & DATE SLICE

- - - - - - - - - - - - - - - -

SERVES 24
- 1¼ cups chopped pitted dates
- ⅔ cup water
- ⅔ cup heavy cream
- ¾ cup light brown sugar
- 1 cup (2 sticks) lightly salted butter, softened, plus extra for greasing
- ½ cup superfine sugar
- 2 teaspoons vanilla bean paste
- 3 eggs
- 1½ cups self-rising flour
- ½ teaspoon baking powder

1. In a saucepan, combine half of the dates and the water and bring to a boil. Reduce the heat and cook very gently for 5 minutes, or until the dates are pulpy. Turn into a bowl and let cool.

2. In a small saucepan, gently heat the cream, brown sugar, and 6 tablespoons (½ stick plus 2 tablespoons) of the butter until the sugar dissolves. Bring to a boil and boil for 5 minutes, or until thickened and caramelized. Let cool.

3. Meanwhile, preheat the oven to 350°F. Grease and line an 11- x 7-inch shallow baking pan.

4. In a bowl, combine the remaining butter, superfine sugar, vanilla bean paste, and eggs, sift in the flour and baking powder, and beat with an electric hand mixer until pale and creamy. Beat in the cooked dates and 6 tablespoons of the caramel mixture.

5. Turn the batter into the prepared pan and level the surface. Sprinkle with the remaining dates. Bake in the oven for 25 minutes, or until just firm. Remove from the oven and spoon the remaining caramel over the top. Bake for an additional 15 minutes, or until the caramel has firmed up. Transfer to a wire rack to cool. Cut into squares to serve.

HONEYED FIG CAKES

SERVES 10

- ½ cup (1 stick) lightly salted butter, softened, plus extra for greasing
- ½ cup superfine sugar
- 2 eggs
- 1 cup ground almonds
- ½ teaspoon almond extract
- ¼ cup self-rising flour, sifted
- Finely grated zest of 1 lemon
- 3 figs, quartered
- 3 tablespoons clear honey
- 1½ tablespoons lemon juice

1. Preheat the oven to 400°F. Grease ten ½-cup dariole molds and line the bottoms with circles of parchment paper. Place on a baking sheet.

2. In a bowl, beat the butter, sugar, eggs, ground almonds, almond extract, flour, and lemon zest together with an electric hand whisk until smooth and creamy.

3. Divide the batter evenly among the prepared molds. Rest a fig quarter in the center of each. Bake in the oven for 15 minutes, or until just firm to the touch. Let cool in the dishes, then transfer to a plate.

4. Mix the honey with the lemon juice, then spoon over the figs.

LEMON-GLAZED CARDAMOM MADELEINES

SERVES 30

- 2 teaspoons cardamom pods
- 3 eggs
- ½ cup superfine sugar
- Finely grated zest of 1 lemon
- 1 cup self-rising flour, plus extra for dusting
- ½ teaspoon baking powder
- ½ cup (1 stick) lightly salted butter, melted, plus extra for greasing

Glaze
- 2 tablespoons lemon juice
- ¾ cup confectioners' sugar, sifted, plus extra for dusting

1. Preheat the oven to 425°F. Grease a madeleine sheet and lightly dust with flour, tapping out the excess.

2. Using a mortar and pestle, crush the cardamom pods to release the seeds. Discard the husks and crush the seeds a little more.

3. In a heatproof bowl set over a saucepan of gently simmering water, beat the eggs, sugar, lemon zest, and crushed cardamom seeds together with an electric hand mixer until pale, creamy, and thick enough for the beaters to leave a trail when lifted from the bowl.

4. Sift in the flour and baking powder and gently fold in with a large metal spoon. Drizzle the melted butter around the edge of the batter and fold the ingredients together until just combined.

5. Spoon the batter into the madeleine sections until about two-thirds full. Keep the remaining batter for more batches depending on the size of your pan. Bake in the oven for 10 minutes, or until risen and golden. Let cool in the pan for 5 minutes, then transfer to a wire rack to cool completely. Make more batches in the same way.

6. Make the glaze. In a bowl, beat the lemon juice into the sugar. Brush over the madeleines and let set. Serve the madeleines dusted with extra confectioners' sugar.

PINK ROSE CUPCAKES

SERVES 12

- 2 cups candied rose petals,
  plus extra to decorate
- Heaping ½ cup superfine sugar
- ½ cup (1 stick) lightly salted butter, softened
- 2 eggs
- 1¼ cups self-rising flour
- ½ teaspoon baking powder
- 1 tablespoon rose water

Frosting
- 1 cup mascarpone cheese
- 1 cup confectioners' sugar
- 1 teaspoon lemon juice
- Few drops pink food coloring (optional)

1. Preheat the oven to 350°F. Line a 12-section mini tart pan with paper cake liners.

2. In a food processor, process the candied rose petals and sugar until the rose petals are chopped into small pieces. Tip into a bowl and add all the remaining cake ingredients. Beat with an electric hand mixer for about 1 minute, or until pale and creamy.

3. Divide the batter evenly among the cake liners. Bake in the oven for 20 minutes, or until risen and just firm to the touch. Transfer to a wire rack to cool.

4. Make the frosting. In a bowl, beat all the frosting ingredients together until smooth. Spread over the tops of the cakes with a small palette knife and decorate with extra candied rose petals.

STRAWBERRY BUTTERFLY CUPCAKES

These pretty little strawberry and vanilla cupcakes are perfect for any princess's tea party. Serve topped with a delicious wild strawberry if possible, otherwise top with a drizzle of homemade strawberry jelly.

SERVES 12

- ½ cup (1 stick) butter, softened
- ½ cup superfine sugar
- 2 eggs, lightly beaten
- 1 teaspoon vanilla extract
- 1 cup self-rising flour
- 1 teaspoon baking powder
- 2 tablespoons milk
- 8 dried strawberries, finely chopped

- 12 fresh wild strawberries or 2 tablespoons good-quality strawberry jelly, warmed, to decorate

Vanilla cream
- ½ cup mascarpone cheese
- 2–3 tablespoons confectioners' sugar
- Seeds scraped from 1 vanilla bean
- 1–2 teaspoons milk, if needed

1. Preheat the oven to 375°F. Line a 12-section cupcake pan with paper cupcake liners.

2. In a large bowl, beat the butter and sugar together until pale and creamy. Gradually beat in the eggs and vanilla extract, a little at a time, beating well after each addition. Gently fold in the flour, baking powder, milk, and dried strawberries with a large metal spoon.

3. Divide the batter evenly among the cupcake liners and bake in the oven for 20–25 minutes, or until risen and firm to touch. Transfer to a wire rack to cool.

4. Make the vanilla cream. In a small bowl, beat the mascarpone, sugar, and vanilla seeds together, adding the milk to loosen if necessary.

5. Use a small, sharp knife to cut a circle of sponge from the top of each cupcake, then cut each top in half. Fill the holes with the vanilla cream and replace the tops so that they resemble butterfly wings. Top each one with either a fresh wild strawberry or a drizzle of strawberry jelly and serve.

RASPBERRY & COCONUT FRIANDS

- - - - - - - - - - - - - - - - - - - -

If you don't have friand pans, you can make this delicious recipe in a shallow muffin pan instead. See the picture on page 92.

SERVES 9

- Vegetable oil, for oiling
- ¾ cup all-purpose flour
- I cup confectioners' sugar
- I cup ground almonds
- ⅔ cup shredded dried coconut
- Finely grated zest of I lemon
- 5 egg whites
- ⅔ cup (I stick plus 2½ tablespoons) unsalted butter, melted
- I cup fresh raspberries

1. Preheat the oven to 400°F. Lightly oil 9 friand pans.

2. Sift the flour and sugar together into a bowl and stir in the ground almonds, coconut, and lemon zest.

3. In a large, thoroughly clean bowl, whip the egg whites with an electric hand whisk until frothy, then fold into the dry ingredients. Add the melted butter and stir until evenly combined.

4. Divide the batter evenly among the prepared pans. Top each friand with a few raspberries and bake in the oven for 18–20 minutes, or until a toothpick inserted into the center comes out clean. Let cool in the pans for 5 minutes, then turn out onto a wire rack to cool completely.

COCONUT CAKES WITH PASSION FRUIT ICING

These rich coconut cakes look especially inviting baked in a mini loaf pan, but you can use a 12-section muffin pan if you prefer.

SERVES 8
- Vegetable oil, for oiling
- ½ cup plus 1 tablespoon (1 stick plus 1 tablespoon) unsalted butter, softened
- ¾ cup superfine sugar
- 2 eggs
- 1 cup self-rising flour
- Scant 1½ cups shredded dried coconut
- 2 tablespoons milk

Frosting
- 1 cup confectioners' sugar, sifted
- 1–2 tablespoons passion fruit pulp

1. Preheat the oven to 325°F. Oil and line the bottoms of an 8-section mini loaf pan.

2. In a food processor, process all the ingredients until evenly blended.

3. Divide the batter evenly among the pan sections and bake in the oven for 30–35 minutes, or until risen and firm to the touch. Let cool in the pan for 5 minutes, then transfer to a wire rack to cool completely.

4. Make the frosting. In a bowl, beat the sugar and passion fruit pulp together until smooth. Place the cakes, still on the wire rack, over a large plate and pour the frosting over, allowing it to drizzle down the sides of the cakes. Let set.

PINK & WHITE LAMINGTONS

SERVES 24

- Butter, for greasing
- 5 eggs
- Generous ¾ cup superfine sugar
- 1 cup self-rising flour
- Scant ½ cup cornstarch
- 1 cup shredded dried coconut

Topping
- 2 cups shredded dried coconut
- 4 cups confectioners' sugar
- ⅓ cup hot water
- ⅓ cup warm milk
- Few drops red food coloring

1. Preheat the oven to 350°F. Grease and line the bottom of a deep 13- x 9-inch baking pan.

2. In a large bowl, beat the eggs with an electric hand mixer for 5 minutes, or until thick, frothy, and tripled in volume. Add the sugar, a tablespoon at a time, beating continuously until the mixture is pale, glossy, and the beaters leave a trail when lifted from the bowl. This will take an additional 5 minutes.

3. Sift in the flour and cornstarch, then gently fold in the coconut until just combined.

4. Turn the batter into the prepared pan and bake in the oven for 25–30 minutes, or until risen, springy to the touch, and a toothpick inserted into the center comes out clean. Turn out onto a wire rack and let cool. Peel off the lining paper and cover the cake with a clean, dry dish towel. Let stand in a cool place for several hours, preferably overnight. Cut the cake into 24 squares.

5. Make the topping. Spread the coconut out on a large, flat plate. In a bowl, beat the sugar, hot water, and warm milk together, then set the bowl over a saucepan of hot water. Using 2 forks, lift 12 of the sponge squares (one at a time) into the sugar mixture to coat. Let the excess mixture drip off, then roll in the coconut to cover. Let set on a wire rack.

6. Add 1–2 drops red food coloring to the sugar mixture, stir well, and then add more, if you like, to turn a deep, vivid pink color. Use to coat the remaining sponge squares in the same way.

FROSTED BANANA BARS

SERVES 16

- ¾ cup (1½ cups) butter, softened
- ¾ cup superfine sugar
- 3 eggs, beaten
- 2 cups self-rising flour
- 1 teaspoon baking powder
- 2 bananas, about 6 oz each with skins on, peeled and coarsely mashed

Frosting
- 4 tablespoons (½ stick) butter
- ¼ cup unsweetened cocoa
- 2¼ cups confectioners' sugar, sifted
- 1–2 tablespoons milk
- Sugar shapes and sprinkles, to decorate

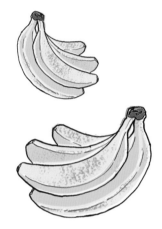

1. Preheat the oven to 350°F. Line a 11- x 7-inch roasting pan.

2. In a bowl, beat the butter and sugar together until pale and creamy. Gradually beat in alternate spoonfuls of the beaten egg and flour until all has been incorporated and the mixture is smooth. Add the baking powder and mashed bananas and mix well.

3. Spoon the batter into the prepared pan and level the surface. Bake in the oven for 25–30 minutes, or until well risen, golden, and springy to the touch. Let cool in the pan.

4. Make the frosting. In a small saucepan, melt the butter, then stir in the cocoa and gently cook for 1 minute. Remove from the heat and mix in the sugar. Return to the heat and gently heat, stirring, until melted and smooth, adding sufficient milk to mix to a smooth, spreadable frosting.

5. Pour the frosting over the top of the cake and spread evenly with a spatula. Sprinkle with sugar shapes and sprinkles and let cool and harden. Lift the cake out of the pan using the lining paper. Cut into bars and peel off the paper.

CHOCOLATE ICED FANCIES

- -

SERVES 16

- ½ cup chopped bittersweet chocolate
- ½ cup (1 stick) lightly salted butter, softened, plus extra for greasing
- ½ cup light brown sugar
- 2 eggs
- ½ cup self-rising flour
- ¼ cup unsweetened cocoa
- ½ cup ground almonds
- 5 tablespoons chocolate hazelnut spread

Frosting
- 7 oz bittersweet chocolate, chopped
- 2 tablespoons dark corn syrup
- 1 tablespoon (⅛ stick) lightly salted butter
- ¼ cup chopped milk chocolate

1. Preheat the oven to 325°F. Grease and line a 6-inch square cake pan. Grease the paper.

2. In a heatproof bowl set over a saucepan of gently simmering water, melt the chocolate.

3. In a separate bowl, beat the butter and sugar together until pale and creamy. Gradually beat in the eggs, a little at a time, beating well after each addition and adding a little of the flour if the batter starts to curdle. Stir in the melted chocolate. Sift in the flour and cocoa, add the ground almonds, and stir in gently.

4. Turn the batter into the prepared pan and level the surface. Bake in the oven for about 20 minutes, or until risen and just firm to the touch. Transfer to a wire rack to cool.

5. Cut the cake into 16 squares and, using a spatula, spread a small mound of chocolate hazelnut spread on the top of each one.

6. Make the frosting. In a saucepan, melt the bittersweet chocolate with the syrup and butter as before until smooth and glossy. Separately melt the milk chocolate. Spoon a little of the bittersweet chocolate mixture over each cake and spread around the sides with a spatula. Using a teaspoon, drizzle lines of milk chocolate over each cake.

MAPLE & PECAN MUFFINS

SERVES 8

- 2½ cups self-rising flour
- I teaspoon baking powder
- ½ cup brown sugar
- I egg
- 3 tablespoons maple syrup
- I cup milk
- 4 tablespoons (½ stick) unsalted butter, melted
- 4 oz white chocolate, finely chopped, plus extra to decorate
- ¾ cup pecans, coarsely chopped, plus extra to decorate

1. Preheat the oven to 400°F. Line a deep 12-section muffin pan with 8 paper muffin liners.

2. Sift the flour and baking powder into a bowl and stir in the sugar.

3. In a separate bowl, beat the egg, maple syrup, milk, and melted butter together. Beat into the dry ingredients until mixed, then fold in the chocolate and pecans.

4. Divide the batter evenly among the muffin liners and top with some extra chopped pecans and chocolate. Bake in the oven for 20–25 minutes, or until risen and golden. Transfer to a wire rack to cool.

APPLE, BRAZIL NUT & FIG MUFFINS

You can make these muffins in classic muffin liners or straight-sided paper liners, whichever you prefer.

SERVES 8

- 2 cups all-purpose flour
- 1½ teaspoons baking powder
- ½ teaspoon ground cinnamon
- Scant ½ cup chopped Brazil nuts
- ¾ cup plus 2 tablespoons granulated sugar
- 1 egg, lightly beaten
- 1¼ cups buttermilk
- 4 tablespoons (½ stick) unsalted butter, melted
- 1 apple, peeled, cored, and diced
- Heaping ⅓ cup dried figs, chopped

1. Preheat the oven to 400°F. Place 8 paper muffin liners on a baking sheet or in a muffin pan.

2. Sift the flour, baking powder, and cinnamon into a bowl, then stir in the nuts and sugar.

3. In a separate bowl, beat the egg, buttermilk, and melted butter together until blended. Stir into the dry ingredients to make a smooth batter. Fold in the apple and figs.

4. Divide the batter evenly among the muffin liners and bake in the oven for 30–35 minutes, or until risen and golden. Transfer the muffins to a wire rack to cool slightly and serve warm.

SWEET CHAMOMILE MUFFINS

- -

Split these chamomile-flavored muffins and serve warm with butter for the perfect snack to enjoy with a soothing cup of tea.

SERVES 12

- 3 tablespoons chamomile tea (either loose leaf or from bags)
- ¾ cup ground almonds
- ½ cup superfine sugar
- 2¼ cups all-purpose flour
- 1 tablespoon baking powder
- Finely grated zest of 1 lemon
- ½ cup golden raisins
- 6 tablespoons (½ stick plus 2 tablespoons) lightly salted butter, melted, plus extra for greasing and to serve
- 2 eggs, lightly beaten
- 1¼ cups buttermilk

1. Preheat the oven to 425°F. Line a 12-section muffin pan with paper muffin liners. Alternately, grease a 12-section nonstick or silicone muffin pan.

2. In a food processor, briefly process the tea, ground almonds, and sugar until combined. Turn into a large bowl and stir in the flour, baking powder, lemon zest, and golden raisins.

3. In a separate bowl, beat the melted butter, eggs, and buttermilk together, then add the mixture to the dry ingredients. Stir the ingredients together until just combined.

4. Divide the batter evenly among the muffin liners or pan sections and bake in the oven for 15–18 minutes, or until risen and pale golden. Transfer the muffins to a wire rack to cool slightly and serve warm, split and buttered.

TIP

- For a more exotic version, replace the chamomile tea with peppermint tea and use 3½ oz chopped white chocolate instead of the golden raisins.

FRUITY LUNCH-BOX MUFFINS

SERVES 12

- ¾ cup all-purpose flour
- ¾ cup whole wheat flour
- 2 teaspoons baking powder
- ⅓ cup superfine sugar
- 2 eggs
- 2 tablespoons mild olive oil or vegetable oil
- 3 tablespoons lightly salted butter, melted
- 2 teaspoons vanilla extract
- ⅔ cup red fruit yogurt, such as strawberry, raspberry, or cherry
- ¾ cup fresh raspberries or ⅔ cup fresh strawberries, hulled and cut into small pieces

1. Preheat the oven to 400°F. Line a 12-section mini tart pan with paper cake liners.

2. In a bowl, combine the flours, baking powder, and sugar.

3. In a pitcher, beat the eggs, oil, melted butter, vanilla extract, and yogurt together with a fork and add to the bowl. Mix gently with a large metal spoon until the ingredients have started to blend together. Scatter with half of the berry pieces and briefly mix until the ingredients are only just combined.

4. Divide the batter evenly among the cake liners. Scatter with the remaining berry pieces. Bake in the oven for 15 minutes, or until well risen and just firm. Transfer to a wire rack to cool.

RUM & RAISIN CHOCOLATE BROWNIES

- - - - - - - - - - - - - - -

SERVES 20

- 3 tablespoons white or dark rum
- ⅔ cup raisins
- 8 oz dark chocolate, broken into pieces
- 1 cup (2 sticks) butter
- 4 eggs
- 1 cup superfine sugar
- ¾ cup self-rising flour
- 1 teaspoon baking powder
- 4 oz white or milk chocolate

1. Preheat the oven to 350°F. Line a 7 x 11-inch roasting pan.

2. Warm the rum, then add the raisins, cover, and let soak for 2 hours or overnight.

3. In a saucepan, gently heat the dark chocolate and butter until melted.

4. In a bowl, beat the eggs and sugar together with an electric hand mixer until pale, creamy, and thick enough for the beaters to leave a trail when lifted from the bowl.

5. Fold the warm chocolate mixture into the egg mixture. Sift in the flour and baking powder, then fold in with a large metal spoon.

6. Pour the batter into the prepared pan and spoon the soaked raisins over the top. Bake in the oven for 25–30 minutes, or until well risen, the top is crusty and cracked, and the center is still slightly soft. Let cool and harden in the pan. Lift out of the pan using the lining paper.

7. In a heatproof bowl set over a saucepan of gently simmering water, melt the white or milk chocolate, then drizzle over the top of the brownie. Let set, then cut into 20 pieces and peel off the lining paper.

FROSTED COFFEE & MACADAMIA BROWNIES

SERVES 12-16

- ¾ cup (1½ sticks) butter, plus extra for greasing
- 6 oz dark chocolate, broken into chunks
- 1½ tablespoons instant coffee dissolved in 1½ tablespoons hot water
- 2 large eggs
- Heaping ¾ cup superfine sugar
- Heaping ⅓ cup self-rising flour
- Pinch of salt
- ⅔ cup coarsely chopped macadamias
- Heaping ⅓ cup grated milk chocolate, to decorate

Frosting
- 5 tablespoons (½ stick plus 1 tablespoon) butter, softened
- 1¾ cups confectioners' sugar, sifted
- 1 teaspoon ground cinnamon
- 1 tablespoon coffee extract

1. Preheat the oven to 400°F. Grease and line the bottom of a 13- x 9-inch brownie pan.

2. In a small, heavy-bottom saucepan, gently heat the butter and dark chocolate with the strong coffee until melted, stirring until smooth. Let cool.

3. In a large bowl, beat the eggs and sugar together, then beat in the chocolate mixture. Add the flour and salt and mix until well combined, then stir in the macadamias.

4. Pour the batter into the prepared pan and bake in the oven for 20 minutes, or until risen but still soft in the center. Let cool completely in the pan.

5. Make the frosting. In a bowl, beat all the frosting ingredients together until smooth. Spread over the cooled brownie, then sprinkle with the grated milk chocolate to decorate. Cut into squares and peel off the lining paper.

ORANGE & ALMOND BLONDIES

Bring the tastes and aromas of the Mediterranean to your kitchen with these golden blondies, full of zesty orange and moist almonds. They make a wonderful, quick dessert served with a small glass of Amaretto liqueur.

SERVES 12-16

- ½ cup plus 3 tablespoons (1 stick plus 3 tablespoons) butter, plus extra for greasing
- 9 oz white chocolate, broken into chunks
- 3 eggs
- ½ cup light brown sugar
- 1 teaspoon orange extract
- 1 teaspoon almond extract
- Finely grated zest of 1 orange
- ¾ cup self-rising flour
- ¾ cup ground almonds
- ½ cup slivered almonds, lightly toasted

1. Preheat the oven to 325°F. Grease and line the bottom of a 9-inch square brownie pan.

2. In a small, heavy-bottom saucepan, gently heat the butter and chocolate until melted, stirring until smooth. Let cool.

3. In a large bowl, beat the eggs, sugar, orange and almond extracts, and orange zest together, then beat in the chocolate mixture. Add the flour and ground almonds and mix until well combined.

4. Pour the batter into the prepared pan, scatter over the slivered almonds, and bake in the oven for 25–30 minutes, or until almost firm and golden. Let cool in the pan, then cut into squares, remove from the lining paper, and lift out with a metal spatula. Serve slightly warm.

TIP

- If not serving straightaway, let cool completely and store in an airtight container between layers of parchment paper.

CINNAMON DOUGHNUTS

As long as you eat these fresh, their flavor and texture far exceed the best bought versions. They're impossible to eat without licking your lips!

SERVES 12

- 2 teaspoons active dry yeast
- ⅓ cup plus 1 tablespoon superfine sugar, plus an extra 1 teaspoon
- ⅓ cup plus 1 tablespoon lukewarm water
- Scant 3 cups bread flour, plus extra for dusting
- 1 egg, beaten
- 4 tablespoons (½ stick) lightly salted butter, melted
- ⅓ cup plus 1 tablespoon lukewarm milk
- Vegetable oil, for oiling and frying

Cinnamon sugar
- ½ teaspoon ground cinnamon
- ½ cup superfine sugar

1. In a small bowl, stir the yeast and the 1 teaspoon sugar into the water and let stand for 10 minutes, or until frothy.

2. In a large bowl, combine the flour with the remaining sugar. Add the egg, melted butter, milk, and yeast mixture and mix to a dough.

3. Turn the dough out on a floured work surface and knead gently for 10 minutes, or until smooth and elastic. Place in a lightly oiled bowl, cover with plastic wrap, and let stand in a warm place for about 1 hour, or until doubled in size.

4. Punch the dough down to deflate it, then divide evenly into 12 pieces. Roll each piece into a ball and space well apart on 2 lightly oiled baking sheets. Cover loosely with oiled plastic wrap and let prove for about 40 minutes, or until doubled in size.

5. Prepare the cinnamon sugar. On a plate, combine the cinnamon and sugar thoroughly.

6. In a large, heavy-bottom pot, heat oil to a depth of 3 inches until a small piece of bread starts to brown in 30 seconds. Fry the doughnuts, a few at a time, for 2–3 minutes, or until puffed and golden. Remove with a slotted spoon and drain on paper towels. Toss in the cinnamon sugar.

ROSE WATER MERINGUE CAKE P125

CAKES WITH A DIFFERENCE

STRAWBERRY SHORTCAKE

Laced with mascarpone-enriched cream and liqueur, this recipe makes a more extravagant strawberry shortcake than many versions. It's perfect for enjoying outdoors in summertime.

SERVES 8

- ¾ cup (1½ sticks) unsalted butter, softened, plus extra for greasing
- ½ cup superfine sugar
- 2 eggs, beaten
- 2 teaspoons vanilla extract
- 1¾ cups self-rising flour
- 1 teaspoon baking powder
- 1¾ cups fresh strawberries
- Scant 1 cup fresh raspberries
- 3 tablespoons Cointreau or other orange-flavored liqueur
- 6 tablespoons red currant jelly
- 1 tablespoon water
- 1 cup plus 2 tablespoons mascarpone cheese
- 1¼ cups heavy cream

1. Preheat the oven to 350°F. Grease a 7-inch round cake pan.

2. In a bowl, beat the butter and sugar together until light and fluffy. Gradually beat in the eggs, a little at a time, beating well after each addition, then beat in the vanilla extract. Sift in the flour and baking powder and stir until combined.

3. Turn the batter into the prepared pan and level the surface. Bake in the oven for 30 minutes, or until just firm to the touch. Transfer to a wire rack to cool. When cool, slice the cake horizontally in half.

4. Meanwhile, hull and halve the strawberries. In a bowl, combine with the raspberries and 1 tablespoon of the liqueur. In a saucepan, gently heat the red currant jelly with the water until it melts.

5. In another bowl, whip the mascarpone, cream, and remaining liqueur together until peaking.

6. Spread the bottom layer of the cake with half of the mascarpone cream and scatter with half of the fruits. Brush with half of the jelly and top with the remaining cake. Finish the top with the remaining cream, fruits, and drizzle over the jelly.

SWEET SAFFRON CAKE

This cake is made using a yeasted dough and is somewhere between a cake and a bread in texture and flavor. It's at its best served very fresh, sliced and buttered.

SERVES 8-10

- I teaspoon saffron threads
- ¾ cup plus 3 tablespoons lukewarm milk
- 2 teaspoons active dry yeast
- ½ cup superfine sugar, plus extra I teaspoon
- 3⅔ cups bread flour, plus extra for dusting

- I egg, beaten
- ¾ cup plus 2 tablespoons (1¾ sticks) salted butter, very soft, plus extra for greasing
- Vegetable oil, for oiling
- 1⅔ cups luxury mixed dried fruit

1. In a small bowl, crumble the saffron threads into the milk, then stir in the yeast and the 1 teaspoon sugar. Let stand for 10 minutes, or until frothy.

2. In a large bowl, combine the flour and remaining sugar. Make a well in the center and add the egg. Slice in the butter and add the yeast mixture. Mix to a soft dough with a round-bladed knife, adding a little extra flour if the dough feels sticky.

3. Turn the dough out onto a floured work surface and knead gently for 10 minutes, or until smooth and elastic. Place in a lightly oiled bowl, cover with plastic wrap, and let stand in a warm place for 1–2 hours, or until doubled in size. Grease a 7-inch round cake pan.

4. Punch the dough down to deflate it and knead in the fruit. Shape into a large round. Drop into the prepared pan, cover loosely with oiled plastic wrap, and let prove for 1 hour, or until doubled in size.

5. Meanwhile, preheat the oven to 375°F.

6. Bake in the oven for 40 minutes, or until deep golden. Remove from the pan and bake directly on the oven rack for an additional 5 minutes. Transfer to a wire rack to cool.

ROSE WATER MERINGUE CAKE

This meringue is beautifully scented with rose water and makes a great dessert or afternoon treat—see the picture on page 120. The meringue can be made in advance, but assemble the cake just before serving.

SERVES 6-8

- Butter, for greasing
- 4 large egg whites
- 1¼ cups superfine sugar
- 2 teaspoons cornstarch
- 1 teaspoon white wine vinegar
- Few drops rose water extract, for the filling and topping
- 1¼ cups lowfat raspberry or strawberry fromage frais or thick yogurt
- ⅔ cup fresh strawberries or raspberries
- Candied rose petals, to decorate

1. Preheat the oven to 300°F. Grease and line the bottoms of two shallow 8-inch round cake pans.

2. In a large, thoroughly clean bowl, whip the egg whites with an electric hand whisk until forming soft peaks. Beat in the sugar, a little at a time, then beat in the cornstarch and vinegar and add a few drops of rose water extract to taste.

3. Divide the meringue mixture among the prepared pans and level the surface. Bake in the oven for 1½ hours, then turn the oven off and let the meringues sit inside until cold.

4. Just before serving, remove the meringues from the pans and peel off the lining paper. Place one meringue round on a serving plate. Spread the fromage frais or yogurt evenly over the meringue and arrange the strawberries or raspberries on top. Place the second meringue round on top and sprinkle with candied rose petals to decorate. Serve immediately, cut into slices.

TIP

- This cake is very low in fat, so ideal for those watching their calorie intake. It's also suitable for those on a wheat- or nut-free diet.

BAKED ALASKA
BIRTHDAY CAKE

- - - - - - - - - - - - - - - - - -

Dim the lights and light the candles. This is an all-time favorite celebration cake and the fresh raspberries make it extra special.

SERVES 6-8

- ¾ cup (1½ sticks) unsalted butter, softened, plus extra for greasing
- ¾ cup granulated sugar
- 3 eggs, beaten
- 1 teaspoon vanilla extract
- 1½ cups self-rising flour, sifted
- 12 oz raspberry jelly
- 1½ cups fresh raspberries
- 4 egg whites
- 1 cup superfine sugar
- 8 scoops of vanilla or your favorite ice cream
- Candles or sparklers, to decorate (optional)

1. Preheat the oven to 350°F. Grease and line the bottom of a deep 8-inch round cake pan.

2. In a large bowl, beat the butter and granulated sugar together until pale and fluffy. Gradually add the eggs, a little at a time, beating well after each addition, then beat in the vanilla extract. Fold in the flour with a large metal spoon, mixing well. Spoon the batter into the prepared pan and level the surface. Bake in the oven for 30–35 minutes, or until risen and golden. Turn out onto a wire rack and let cool.

3. Increase the oven temperature to 425°F. Slice the cake horizontally in half. Place the bottom cake layer on a baking sheet and spread with the jelly. Place the second cake layer on top. Arrange the raspberries on top of the cake.

4. In a large, thoroughly clean bowl, whip the egg whites with an electric hand whisk until forming stiff peaks. Beat in in the superfine sugar, a little at a time, until thick and glossy.

5. Place the scoops of ice cream over the raspberries to cover. Spread the meringue mixture evenly over the ice cream and side of the sponge so that everything is covered. Bake in the oven for 8–10 minutes. Decorate with birthday candles or sparklers, if you like, and serve immediately in slices.

NEW YORK CHEESECAKE

You can dress this Big Apple classic up or down as you like. Serve it plain or topped with fruit compote.

SERVES 12-14

- 7 oz graham crackers, crushed
- 4 tablespoons (½ stick) unsalted butter, melted, plus extra for greasing
- 4 x 8-oz packages cream cheese
- Pinch of salt
- 1½ cups superfine sugar
- 1 cup sour cream
- 2 teaspoons vanilla extract
- 1 tablespoon finely grated lemon zest
- 1 tablespoon lemon juice
- 4 eggs, beaten
- 2 egg yolks

1. Preheat the oven to 300°F. Grease a 9-inch round springform cake pan.

2. In a bowl, mix the graham cracker crumbs and melted butter together, then press evenly onto the bottom of the prepared pan. Bake in the oven for 10 minutes, or until lightly browned. Let cool.

3. In a separate bowl, beat the cream cheese until soft and smooth. Add the salt and sugar and beat for 1 minute. Add the sour cream, vanilla extract, and lemon zest and juice and beat for an additional 1 minute. Add the eggs and egg yolks and beat until well combined.

4. Pour the mixture evenly over the graham cracker crust in the pan. Bake in the oven for 45–50 minutes, or until the edge is set but the center is still slightly soft. Turn off the oven and let the cheesecake sit inside, with the door ajar, for 45 minutes.

5. Remove the cheesecake from the oven and cool to room temperature. Remove from the pan and place on a serving plate. Cover with foil and chill for at least 4 hours, or preferably overnight. Serve in slices.

PEACH & ALMOND ROULADE

- - - - - - - - - - - - - - - -

Make this gorgeous roulade when peaches are juicy and at their absolute best. Leave any that are slightly underripe in the fruit bowl for a couple of days to accelerate ripening.

SERVES 8

- Butter, for greasing
- 5 eggs, separated
- ⅔ cup superfine sugar, plus extra for dusting
- 4 oz white almond paste, grated
- 3 tablespoons all-purpose flour
- 2 tablespoons brandy or almond liqueur
- 1¼ cups crème fraîche or equal quantities sour cream and whipping cream
- 2 ripe peaches, pitted and thinly sliced

1. Preheat the oven to 350°F. Grease and line a 13- x 9-inch jelly roll pan. Grease the paper.

2. In a large bowl, beat the egg yolks and sugar together with an electric hand mixer until pale and creamy. Beat in the almond paste, then stir in the flour. Clean the beaters thoroughly.

3. In a separate, thoroughly clean bowl, whip the egg whites with the hand mixer until peaking. Fold into the almond mixture with a large metal spoon until combined.

4. Turn the batter into the prepared pan and gently spread into the corners. Bake in the oven for 20 minutes, or until risen and firm to the touch.

5. Meanwhile, sprinkle a sheet of parchment paper with a little sugar.

6. Turn the cooked sponge out onto the sugared paper and let cool.

7. Drizzle the liqueur over the sponge. Spread the crème fraîche or sour cream and cream mixture over the sponge and scatter with the peaches. Roll up, starting from a short side and using the paper to help you, and transfer, seam-side down, to a serving plate. Chill until ready to serve.

TORTE WITH FIVE-SPICE SYRUP

Unlike most rich chocolate cakes, this one is "poached" in the oven so it stays amazingly moist. Drizzle with the syrup on the serving plates.

SERVES 12

- 1⅓ cup plus 1 tablespoon dark brown sugar
- ⅔ cup plus 2 tablespoons water
- 11 oz dark chocolate, chopped
- 1 cup (2 sticks) unsalted butter, diced, plus extra for greasing
- 6 eggs
- 2 teaspoons five-spice powder
- Unsweetened cocoa, for dusting
- Chocolate ribbons, to decorate

1. Preheat the oven to 325°F. Grease and line a 9-inch round cake pan (don't use a loose-bottom pan). Grease the paper.

2. In a saucepan, dissolve ¾ cup of the sugar in ⅓ cup plus 1 tablespoon water. Bring to a boil and boil for 2 minutes, or until slightly syrupy. Remove from the heat, add the chocolate and butter, and let stand until melted, stirring frequently. (If the mixture cools before the chocolate and butter have melted, heat it through very gently.)

3. In a large, thoroughly clean bowl, whip the eggs and another ⅓ cup plus 1 tablespoon of the sugar together with an electric hand mixer until pale, creamy, and thick enough for the beaters to leave a trail when lifted from the bowl. Fold into the cooled chocolate mixture with a large metal spoon.

4. Pour it into the prepared pan. Sit the pan in a roasting pan and pour in very hot water to a depth of 1½ inches. Bake in the oven for about 1 hour, or until the cake is risen and wobbly in the center. Lift the cake pan from the roasting pan and let cool completely.

5. In a small saucepan, gently heat the remaining sugar with ⅓ cup plus 1 tablespoon water until the sugar dissolves. Bring to a boil and boil rapidly for 3 minutes. Stir in the five-spice powder and simmer for 1 minute more.

6. Remove the cake from the pan and decorate with chocolate ribbons. Dust with cocoa and serve in wedges with the syrup spooned over.

OLIVE OIL CAKE

Use an extra-virgin olive oil for this cake but make sure it's a mild one. This delicious cake is also good served with fresh fruit.

SERVES 10-12

- 1¼ cups unrefined superfine sugar
- Finely grated zest of 2 lemons
- 4 eggs, beaten
- 1 cup gluten-free flour
- 2 teaspoons gluten-free baking powder
- ½ cup ground almonds
- 5 tablespoons rice milk
- ⅔ cup mild extra-virgin olive oil
- 6 tablespoons dairy-free margarine, melted, plus extra for greasing
- Juice of 1 lemon
- ¼ cup pine nuts, lightly toasted

1. Preheat the oven to 350°F. Grease and line a 9-inch round springform cake pan.

2. In a large bowl, whip the sugar, lemon zest, and eggs together with an electric hand mixer until pale, creamy, and thick enough for the beaters to leave a trail when lifted from the bowl.

3. Sift the flour and baking powder into a separate bowl, then stir in the ground almonds.

4. Beat the rice milk, oil, melted margarine, and lemon juice into the egg mixture, then fold in the flour mixture with a large metal spoon until just combined.

5. Pour the batter evenly into the prepared pan and sprinkle with the pine nuts. Bake in the oven for 30–40 minutes, or until golden brown and firm to the touch. Let cool completely in the pan, then turn out and serve in slices.

SCENTED TEA LOAF

- -

Lady Grey tea has a lovely scent of orange and lemon peel, but if you can't find it, you can substitute Earl Grey tea. This cake tastes even better after a few days.

SERVES 12-14

- ½ cup dairy-free margarine, plus extra for greasing
- 1 cup unrefined superfine sugar
- 1 cup strong brewed Lady Grey tea
- 1½ cups luxury mixed dried fruit
- ⅔ cup rice flour
- ⅔ cup potato flour
- 2 teaspoons gluten-free baking powder
- Finely grated zest and juice of 1 orange
- Finely grated zest of 1 lemon
- 1 egg, beaten
- 2 tablespoons strained apricot jelly, warmed

1. Preheat the oven to 350°F. Grease and line a 10-inch loaf pan.

2. In a saucepan, bring the margarine, sugar, tea, and dried fruit to a boil. Simmer gently for 5 minutes, stirring occasionally. Remove from the heat and let cool for 15 minutes.

3. Sift the flours and baking powder into a bowl. Add the flour mixture, orange zest and juice, lemon zest, and egg to the fruit mixture and stir to mix well.

4. Pour the batter evenly into the prepared pan and bake in the oven for 1-1½ hours, or until well risen and firm to the touch. Brush the top of the hot cake with the apricot jelly.

5. Cool in the pan for about 20 minutes, then turn out onto a wire rack and let cool completely. Serve in slices.

TIP

• This cake is suitable for serving to those on gluten-free, wheat-free, nut-free, and dairy-free diets. All gluten-free cakes can be improved by adding ¼ teaspoon xanthan gum to every ⅔ cup flour. Readily available from health food stores, it helps increase volume and how long you can keep it for.

ORANGE CAKE WITH ROSEMARY GLAZE

- -

This is a tasty cut-and-come-again cake, suitable for those on both dairy-free and gluten free diets, is good served with either coffee or tea.

SERVES 8-10

- 1 cup gluten-free flour
- 2 tablespoons rice flour
- ¼ teaspoon baking soda
- ¼ teaspoon gluten-free baking powder
- Scant ½ cup dairy-free margarine, plus extra for greasing
- 1 cup unrefined superfine or granulated sugar
- Finely grated zest of 1 orange
- 2 eggs, beaten

- ½ teaspoon vanilla extract
- 3 tablespoons orange juice
- 3 tablespoons rice milk
- 5 tablespoons coconut milk

Syrup
- 5 tablespoons orange juice
- 2 tablespoons unrefined superfine sugar
- Sprig of fresh rosemary, washed and patted dry

1. Preheat the oven to 350°F. Grease and line a 5-inch loaf pan.

2. Sift the flours, baking soda, and baking powder into a bowl. In a separate bowl, beat the margarine, sugar, and orange zest together. Gradually add the eggs, a little at a time, beating well after each addition.

3. In another bowl, combine the vanilla extract, orange juice, rice milk, and coconut milk. Stir thoroughly into the egg mixture alternately with the flour mixture. Don't overmix.

4. Spoon the batter into the prepared pan and level the surface. Bake in the oven for about 1 hour, or until a skewer inserted into the center comes out clean.

5. Meanwhile, make the syrup. Place the orange juice and sugar in a small saucepan. Strip the leaves from the sprig of rosemary and add to the pan. Bring to a boil, stirring, and boil for about 2 minutes, or until syrupy.

6. Prick the top of the hot cake all over with a toothpick or fork and slowly pour over the syrup. Let cool completely in the pan, then turn out and serve in slices.

PEAR & MARZIPAN LOAF

- - - - - - - - - - - - - - - - - - -

The combination of sticky pear and melting marzipan tastes just fabulous in this loaf.

SERVES 12

- 1 cup golden raisins
- 1½ cups dried pears, chopped
- 2 tablespoons apple juice
- Few drops almond extract
- 1 cup plus 2 tablespoons marzipan, cut into small cubes and frozen
- 3 tablespoons ground almonds
- 6 tablespoons granulated sugar
- 7 tablespoons (½ stick plus 3 tablespoons) butter, softened, plus extra for greasing
- 2 eggs, beaten
- 1 cup rice flour

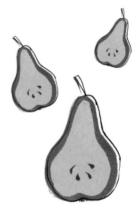

1. In a nonmetallic bowl, combine the golden raisins, pears, apple juice, and almond extract. Cover and let soak overnight.

2. Preheat the oven to 300°F. Grease and line a 2-pound loaf pan.

3. In a large bowl, beat all the remaining ingredients together, stirring in the soaked fruit until well combined.

4. Spoon the mixture into the prepared pan and bake in oven for 1–1½ hours, or until a toothpick inserted into the center comes out clean. Transfer to a wire rack to cool.

FUDGY APPLE LOAF

Gooey fudge and moist apple make this loaf a real family favorite.

SERVES 12

- 1 cup granulated sugar
- 3 eggs
- 2½ cups brown rice flour
- 1 teaspoon gluten-free baking powder
- ¾ cup plus 2 tablespoons (1¾ sticks) butter, melted, plus extra for greasing
- Few drops vanilla extract
- 2 dessert apples, peeled, cored, and chopped

Fudge
- 13-oz can condensed milk
- ⅔ cup milk
- 2 cups light brown sugar
- 7 tablespoons (½ stick plus 3 tablespoons) butter

1. Make the fudge. In a heavy-bottom saucepan, gently heat all the fudge ingredients until the sugar dissolves. Bring to a boil and boil for about 10 minutes, or until the mixture reaches 230°F on a sugar thermometer. Remove from the heat and beat for 5 minutes, then pour into a pan and let cool.

2. Preheat the oven to 350°F. Grease and line a 2-pound loaf pan.

3. In a large bowl, whip the sugar and eggs together with an electric hand mixer until pale, creamy, and thick enough for the beaters to leave a trail when lifted from the bowl. Sift in the flour and baking powder, then fold in with the melted butter, vanilla extract, two-thirds of the apple, and three-fourths of the fudge, chopped, with a large metal spoon.

4. Spoon the batter into the prepared pan, then scatter over the remaining apple and chopped fudge. Bake in the oven for about 1½ hours, or until golden and firm to touch. Transfer to a wire rack to cool.

OVEN SCONES

These scones are very quick and easy to make. Serve them fresh from the oven—make a pot of tea while they're are baking.

SERVES 12

- 2 cups all-purpose white or whole wheat flour, plus extra for dusting, and to serve (optional)
- ½ teaspoon salt
- 4 teaspoons baking powder
- 2–4 tablespoons (¼–½ stick) butter or margarine, plus extra to serve
- ⅔ cup milk, plus extra to glaze (optional)
- Water to thin if needed

To serve
- Thick cream
- Jam

1. Preheat the oven to 450°F. Warm a baking sheet in the oven.

2. Sift the flour, salt, and baking powder into a bowl. Cut the fat into the flour and rub in with the fingertips until the mixture resembles fine bread crumbs.

3. Make a well in the center, pour in the milk, and mix to a soft spongy dough, adding a little water if necessary.

4. Turn the dough out onto a well-floured work surface and knead quickly and lightly. Roll out the dough with a floured rolling pin or flatten with floured hands until ¾ inch thick. Cut into circles with a 2½-inch floured cookie cutter or a glass. Place the scones on the warm baking sheet. Shape the remaining dough into a ball and flatten into a circle, then cut out more scones and place on the baking sheet.

5. Brush the scones with milk for a glazed finish or rub them with flour for a soft crust. Bake near the top of the oven for 7–10 minutes, or until well risen and golden on top. Split and spread with butter, cream, and jam to serve.

BLUEBERRY CHEESECAKE CUPCAKES

These colorful cupcakes are bursting with blueberries and covered with a divine, slightly chewy vanilla cheesecake topping.

SERVES 12

- 5 tablespoons (½ stick plus 1 tablespoon) butter, softened
- ⅓ cup superfine sugar
- 2 eggs, lightly beaten
- 1¼ cups all-purpose flour
- 1 teaspoon baking powder
- Pinch of salt

- 2–3 tablespoons milk
- ⅔ cup fresh or frozen blueberries

Cheesecake filling
- 1 cup mascarpone cheese
- ⅔ cup granulated sugar
- Seeds scraped from 1 vanilla bean
- 1 egg

1. Preheat the oven to 350°F. Line a 12-section cupcake pan with paper cupcake liners.

2. Make the cheesecake filling. In a bowl, beat all the filling ingredients together until smooth.

3. In a separate large bowl, beat the butter and sugar together until pale and creamy. Gradually beat in the eggs, a little at a time, beating well and adding a tablespoon of the flour after each addition.

4. Sift in the remaining flour, baking powder, and salt and gently fold in with a large metal spoon, adding sufficient milk to create a good dropping consistency. Stir in the blueberries.

5. Spoon the batter evenly into the cupcake liners, leaving a dip in the center of each. Pour the cheesecake filling over each cupcake and bake in the oven for 30–35 minutes, or until risen and the cheesecake topping is golden.

6. Let the cupcakes cool in the pan for 2–3 minutes, then transfer to a wire rack. Serve slightly warm or cold.

TEA CAKES

SERVES 8

- 4 cups all-purpose flour, plus extra for dusting
- 1 teaspoon salt
- 2 teaspoons superfine or granulated sugar, plus extra for creaming the yeast
- ⅔ cup currants
- 1 oz fresh yeast
- 1¼ cups warm milk
- Butter, melted, for brushing, plus extra for greasing and to serve

1. Sift the flour and salt into a bowl. Stir in the sugar and currants.

2. Cream the yeast with a little extra sugar and some of the warm milk.

3. Make a well in the center of the dry ingredients, pour in the yeast mixture, and let stand in a warm place for 10 minutes. Add the remaining milk to the yeast mixture and mix to a light dough.

4. Turn the dough out on a lightly floured work surface and knead well. Return to the bowl, cover with plastic wrap or a clean dish towel, and let stand in a warm place for about 1–1½ hours, or until doubled in size.

5. Punch the dough down to deflate it, then divide evenly into 8 pieces. Roll and shape each piece into a round cake. Prick each one with a fork. Transfer the tea cakes to a greased baking sheet, cover with a clean dish towel, and let prove in a warm place for 30 minutes.

6. Meanwhile, preheat the oven to 425°F.

7. Bake the tea cakes in the oven for 10–12 minutes. Remove from the oven, brush with melted butter, and bake for an additional 10 minutes. Split, toast lightly, and spread with butter to serve.

ROCK BUNS

These are quick and easy to make and lovely when eaten freshly baked. Don't let them hang around for too long though, or they will live up to their otherwise inappropriate name.

SERVES 20

- ½ cup plus 1 tablespoon (1 stick plus 1 tablespoon) unsalted butter, softened, plus extra for greasing
- ½ cup unrefined superfine sugar
- 1¾ cups self-rising flour
- 1 teaspoon ground ginger
- 1 teaspoon ground cinnamon
- 1 egg, beaten
- ⅔ cup milk
- ⅔ cup golden raisins
- ½ cup currants
- 2 oz white sugar cubes

1. Preheat the oven to 375°F. Grease 2 baking sheets.

2. In a bowl, beat the butter and sugar together until light and fluffy. Stir in the flour, spices, egg, and milk and mix to a soft dough. Stir in the dried fruit.

3. Place dessertspoonfuls of the batter onto the prepared baking sheets, spacing them slightly apart.

4. Place the sugar cubes in a plastic bag and lightly crush with a rolling pin. Scatter over the buns and bake in the oven for about 15 minutes, or until risen and golden. Transfer to a wire rack to cool.

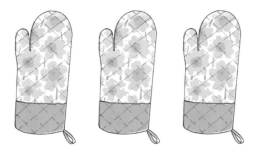

BABY
PANETTONES

We usually see beautifully boxed panettone breads hanging in the deli, particularly during the festive season. Once cooled, these mini versions look lovely rewrapped in fresh paper.

SERVES 8

- ¾ cup lukewarm milk
- 2 teaspoons active dry yeast
- ⅔ cup superfine sugar, plus 1 teaspoon
- 5 cups plus 1 tablespoon bread flour, plus extra if needed and for dusting
- 4 large eggs, plus 2 yolks
- 2 teaspoons vanilla extract
- Finely grated zest of 2 lemons
- ¾ cup (1½ sticks) salted butter, very soft, cut into small pieces, plus extra for greasing
- Vegetable oil, for oiling
- Scant 1¼ cups mixed dried fruit

1. Grease and line the sides of eight 14-ounce cleaned food cans. Grease the paper.

2. Warm a large bowl, then add the milk and stir in the yeast and the 1 teaspoon sugar. Let stand for 10 minutes, or until frothy. Stir in a heaping ⅔ cup of the flour. Cover with plastic wrap and let stand for 30 minutes.

3. Add the eggs and yolks, the remaining flour and sugar, the vanilla extract, lemon zest, and butter. Mix well with a round-bladed knife to make a soft dough, adding a little more flour if the dough feels sticky.

4. Turn the dough out on a lightly floured work surface and knead until smooth and elastic. Transfer to a lightly oiled bowl, cover with plastic wrap, and let stand in a warm place for 2–4 hours, or until doubled in size.

5. Punch down the dough to deflate it, then knead in the fruit. Cut into 8 pieces and drop into the prepared cans. Cover and let prove until the dough almost reaches the rims.

6. Meanwhile, preheat the oven to 400°F.

7. Bake in the oven for 20–25 minutes, or until risen and golden. Let cool in the cans for 5 minutes, then transfer to a wire to cool completely.

STRAWBERRY MARGARITA CUPCAKES

- - - - - - - - - - - - - - - -

SERVES 12

- ½ cup dried strawberries
- 6 tablespoons tequila
- ½ cup (1 stick) lightly salted butter, softened
- Heaping ½ cup superfine sugar
- Finely grated zest and juice of 1 lime
- 2 eggs
- 1¼ cups self-rising flour
- ½ teaspoon baking powder

To finish
- Few drops red food coloring
- ¼ cup superfine sugar
- ⅔ cup heavy cream
- 12 fresh strawberries

1. Coarsely chop the dried strawberries. In a small bowl, combine with the tequila. Cover and let soak for at least 2 hours, or until the strawberries have plumped.

2. Preheat the oven to 350°F. Line a 12-section mini tart pan with paper cake liners.

3. Drain the soaked strawberries, reserving the tequila.

4. In a large bowl, beat the butter, sugar, lime zest, eggs, flour, and baking powder together with an electric hand mixer for about 1 minute, or until light and creamy. Stir in the soaked strawberries.

4. Divide the batter evenly among the cake liners and bake in the oven for 20 minutes, or until risen and just firm to the touch. Transfer to a wire rack to cool.

5. In a small bowl, work the food coloring into the sugar with the back of a teaspoon. Lightly brush the edges of the cakes with lime juice and roll the rims in the colored sugar. Mix the remaining lime juice with the reserved tequila. Pierce the cakes all over with a toothpick and drizzle over the juice mixture.

6. In a bowl, whip the cream until just beginning to hold its shape, then pipe or spoon over the cakes. Decorate each with a whole fresh strawberry.

HOT & SPICY CUPCAKES

SERVES 12

- 1 medium-strength red chile, seeded and finely chopped
- ½ cup (1 stick) lightly salted butter, softened
- ¾ cup superfine sugar
- 2 eggs
- 1¼ cups self-rising flour
- ½ teaspoon baking powder
- 1 cup chopped soft dried mango
- 2 tablespoons water
- 5 tablespoons vodka
- ⅔ cup confectioners' sugar
- Finely grated zest of 1 lime

1. Preheat the oven to 350°F. Line a 12-section mini tart pan with paper cake liners.

2. In a bowl, beat the chopped chile, butter, ½ cup of the superfine sugar, the eggs, flour, and baking powder with an electric hand mixer for about 1 minute, or until light and creamy. Stir in the mango.

3. Divide the batter among the cake liners, then place a halved chile across the top of each cake. Bake in the oven for 20 minutes, or until risen and just firm to the touch. Transfer to a wire rack to cool.

4. In a small saucepan, gently heat the remaining superfine sugar and water until the sugar dissolves. Bring to a boil and boil for 3–4 minutes, or until thickened and syrupy. Stir in 4 tablespoons of the vodka (be careful because the mixture will splutter) and heat until smooth.

5. Pierce the tops of the cupcakes with a toothpick and drizzle over the syrup. Blend the remaining vodka with the confectioners' sugar to make a thin paste and drizzle over the cakes. Sprinkle with the lime zest.

CHILE CORNMEAL CAKES

These cakes look wonderfully exotic with the chiles on the top—see page 155 for a picture of the finished cakes.

SERVES 12

- ⅔ cup cornmeal
- ¼ cup superfine sugar
- ½ teaspoon baking powder
- ⅓ cup ground almonds
- 2 tablespoons olive oil
- 2 eggs
- Juice of 1 lime
- 1 medium-strength red chile, seeded and finely sliced, plus 6 small red chiles, halved lengthwise to decorate

Frosting
- 2 limes
- 1 cup fondant sugar

1. Preheat the oven to 350°F. Place 16 mini silicone muffin cups on a baking sheet.

2. In a bowl, combine the cornmeal, sugar, baking powder, and ground almonds. In a separate bowl, beat the oil, eggs, lime juice, and half of the chile together. Add to the dry ingredients and stir to make a smooth paste.

3. Divide the batter evenly among the muffin cups and add half a chile to the top of each. Bake in the oven for 10 minutes, or until pale golden around the edges. Let cool in the cups.

4. Make the frosting. Use a citrus zester to pare thin curls of zest from the limes. Squeeze and measure 4 teaspoons of the juice.

5. In a bowl, beat the sugar with the lime juice to give a consistency that thinly coats the back of the spoon, adding a bit more juice if necessary. Stir in the lime zest. Drizzle a small amount of frosting on each cake.

SPICED CORN & BACON MUFFINS

SERVES 12

- 2 corn on the cobs
- 4 slices smoked bacon, finely chopped
- 1 small onion, finely chopped
- 2½ cups cornmeal
- 1 tablespoon baking powder
- ½ teaspoon salt
- 1½ teaspoons dried red pepper flakes
- 1 teaspoon cumin seeds, crushed
- ¼ cup chopped fresh cilantro
- 2 eggs
- 5 tablespoons (½ stick plus 1 tablespoon) lightly salted butter, melted
- Scant 1 cup milk

1. In a large saucepan of boiling water, cook the corn cobs for 5 minutes. Drain and let cool. Using a knife, strip the kernels away from the cobs.

2. Heat a small, dry skillet and gently pan-fry the bacon and onion, stirring frequently, until the bacon is turning crisp and golden. Let cool.

3. Meanwhile, preheat the oven to 425°F. Line a 12-section muffin pan with paper muffin liners.

4. In a bowl, combine the cornmeal, baking powder, salt, red pepper flakes, cumin, and cilantro. Stir in the bacon, onion, and corn.

5. In a pitcher, beat the eggs with the melted butter and milk and add to the dry ingredients. Gently stir the ingredients together until they are only just combined.

6. Divide the batter evenly among the cake liners and bake in the oven for 15 minutes, or until risen and pale golden. Transfer to a wire rack to cool. Serve warm or cold.

PINK ROSE CUPCAKES P102

FROSTINGS

BUTTERCREAM

The best buttercream is very soft and fluffy with a flavor that's not too overpoweringly sweet. This recipe makes enough to sandwich and spread over the top of a 7–8-inch cake, or to cover the top and side.

- 7 tablespoons (½ stick plus 3 tablespoons) unsalted butter, softened
- 1¼ cups confectioners' sugar

1. In a bowl, beat the butter with a little of the sugar until smooth.

2. Add the remaining sugar and beat until pale and fluffy. Add a few drops of boiling water and beat for a few moments more.

TIP

- For a coffee-flavored alternative, dissolve 1 tablespoon instant espresso powder in 2 teaspoons hot water, then beat into the buttercream.

GLACÉ ICING

Using lemon or lime juice instead of water in glacé icing gives a welcome tang that helps balance the sweetness of the sugar. Most confectioners' sugars are free flowing, rather than caking together in lumps in the package. If you open a package that's a bit lumpy, sift it first.
This recipe makes enough to thinly cover the top of a 7–8-inch cake.

- ⅔ cup confectioners' sugar
- 2 teaspoons lemon or lime juice

1. Place the sugar in a bowl, sifting it first if it's at all lumpy.

2. Add the juice and beat until smooth.

3. Spread over the warm or cooled cake, depending on the recipe.

CREAM CHEESE FROSTING

This is a lovely tangy frosting with plenty of flavor, and it's great for anyone who doesn't like intensely sugary spreads. Taste for sweetness once it's whisked—you can easily beat in more sugar to taste if it's not sweet enough. This recipe makes enough to sandwich and spread over the top of a 7–8-inch cake or to cover the top and side.

- ¾ cup plus 2 tablespoons cream cheese
- 1–2 teaspoons lime or lemon juice
- ⅔ cup confectioners' sugar

1. In a bowl, beat the cream cheese until softened and smooth. Beat in 1 teaspoon of the juice.

2. Add the sugar and beat until smooth, adding a little more juice if the mixture is very firm.

TIP

- You can use mascarpone cheese instead of cream cheese. Chill the frosting for an hour if it's too soft to spread.

COCONUT FROSTING

This seriously rich frosting is perfect for spreading over the Angel Cake on page 65, but it's also great for adding a lively flavor to a plain Victoria sandwich (see page 14), in which case you could match the frosting's tropical theme by sandwiching the cake with a tropical fruit jam. This recipe makes enough to cover the top and side of a 7–8-inch cake.

- ⅓ cup light cream
- 2 oz creamed coconut, chopped
- 2–3 teaspoons lemon or lime juice
- 2½ cups confectioners' sugar

1. In a small saucepan, gently heat the cream until the coconut melts.

2. Turn into a bowl and beat in the juice and sugar until thick and smooth.

CHOCOLATE GANACHE

A blend of cream and chocolate, ganache is pure indulgence. Used to top chocolate sponges or cupcakes, it's worth making before you start the cake, as it can take a while to set. To make a white chocolate ganache, see page 72. This recipe makes enough to cover the top of a 7–8-inch cake.

- 1¼ cups heavy cream
- 10 oz dark chocolate, chopped

1 In a small saucepan, heat the cream until just bubbling around the edge. Remove from the heat and stir in the chocolate.

2. Turn into a bowl and stir frequently until the chocolate has melted.

3. Cover and chill until the mixture holds its shape before spreading.

LEMON CREAM

- -

This recipe makes enough to cover the top of a 7–8-inch cake.

- ¾ cup plus 1 tablespoon heavy cream
- 2 tablespoons lemon curd

1. In a bowl, lightly whip the cream until it forms soft peaks.

2. Gently mix in the lemon curd.

3. Spread the frosting over the cake and chill until ready to serve.

WHITE CHOCOLATE FUDGE FROSTING

- -

This recipe makes enough to cover 12 small cakes.

- 7 oz white chocolate, chopped
- 5 tablespoons milk
- 1½ cups confectioners' sugar

1. In a heatproof bowl set over a saucepan of gently simmering water, melt the chocolate with the milk, stirring frequently.

2. Remove from the heat and stir in the sugar until smooth.

3. Use the frosting while still warm.

CHILE CORNMEAL CAKES P145

INDEX

GLOSSARY

- All-purpose flour = **plain flour**
- Bittersweet chocolate = **dark chocolate**
- Cilantro = **coriander**
- Confectioners' sugar = **icing sugar**
- Corn syrup = **golden syrup**
- Cornstarch = **cornflour**
- Decorating tip = **nozzle**
- Jelly roll pan = **Swiss roll tin**
- Heavy cream = **double cream**
- Plastic wrap = **cling film**
- Self rising flour = **self raising flour**
- Semisweet chocolate = plain chocolate
- Superfine sugar = caster sugar
- Zucchini = courgette

PICTURE CREDITS